home living workbooks

pillows

home living workbooks

pillows

KatrinCargill

photography by **James Merrell**

Clarkson Potter/Publishers
New York

Originally published in Great Britain in 1996 by Ryland Peters & Small.

Published by Clarkson N. Potter/Publishers, 201 East 50th Street, New York, New York 10022. Member of the Crown Publishing Group.

Random House, Inc. New York, Toronto, London, Sydney, Auckland.

http://www.randomhouse.com/

CLARKSON N. POTTER, POTTER, and colophon are trademarks of Clarkson N. Potter, Inc.

Printed in Hong Kong.

Library of Congress Cataloging-in-Publication Data is available upon request.

ISBN 0-517-70672-5

10 9 8 7 6 5 4 3 2 1

First American Edition

contents

a whole book about pillows? A bit one track? Maybe, but I

for one love to prop my tired back against a soft, comfortable throw pillow,

I adore using two or three sublimely soft pillows for a relaxing Sunday read

of the newspapers, and other more ebullient and energetic members of my

family like to indulge in fights with some of our pillows. Consequently we

wear pillows out on a fairly regular basis, and sad as I am to see a frayed

favorite bite the dust, it does open up possibilities for new ideas and new

fabrics and trimmings. I keep a large box of cuttings of all my favorite

fabrics and an even larger box of remnants, antique textiles, and other bits

and pieces, and I love to put ideas together and toss a fresh new pillow on

the couch.

Pillows not only serve the purpose of softening a seat or supporting a back,

but can also act as a foil for color in a room. A plain, neutral sofa or

armchair can be altered dramatically by the addition of a few primary-

colored pillows, or some soft muted ones. A wooden bench can take on a

new look and added comfort with a cushion. Pillows don't need to be plain

squares of color - be bold and try circles and other shapes, mix colors and

patterns, embroider a little pillow with someone's initials as a present, or

make a mattress-pad cushion for a hard stool. The possibilities are endless,

and this book offers inspiration as well as solid instructions for making

pillows yourself.

Katrin Cargill

left A rectangular pillow in green and white striped cotton has an exaggerated padded border in plain green brushed cotton.

below A trio of shapes: a heart outlined with a heavy chenille fringe; a tailored boxed triangle emphasized by thin dark piping; and a narrow bolster in a woven linen check.

shapes

Mention the word pillow and what probably springs to mind is a typical square shape. Although there are some differently shaped pillows available ready-made, if you are prepared to hunt for more unusual pillow forms, or better still, make up your own shaped ones by simply stuffing a casing you have sewn yourself, then you can create original pillows in any number of shapes.

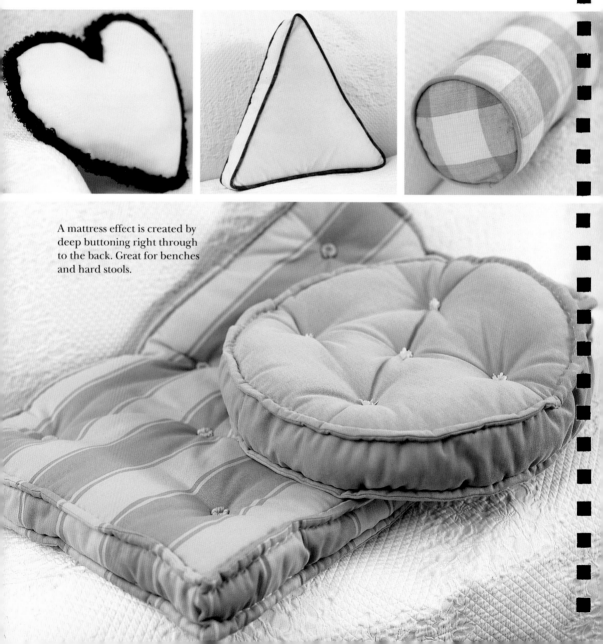

A mattress effect is created by deep buttoning right through to the back. Great for benches and hard stools.

above Star struck: this three-dimensional shape can provide the only pattern on a plain sofa or chair.

left from top A ball fringe in a deeper contrasting color livens up a plain fabric. Cubes made from brushed cotton are fun in a modern room. Green plaid squares echo the square shape of this pillow which has Turkish corners caught together with a darker green thin piping. A football-shaped pillow with contrasting piping, constructed from four panels, looks ready to fly through the air. Square of squares: a woven checked linen and viscose fabric with a tightly gathered little ruffled edge.

below A rectangle of horizontal stripes in cotton outlined with bottle-green wool ball fringe.

the star

This shape can really provide an unusual accent to a decorative scheme. It may not be one to curl up with for cozy reading, but a strongly contrasting colored star or two can provide a wonderful accent in any room. It may be tricky to find this shape, but it is easy to make your own using a satisfyingly simple mathematical process. This one is made from cotton check with an embroidered floral motif and is thinly piped in a contrasting color.

materials & equipment

⅞ yard checked cotton, 60 inches wide

contrasting fabric to make 96 inches of piping

2¾ yards extra thin piping cord, ⅛-inch wide

fiberfill or other stuffing

a sheet of paper 24 x 24 inches

protractor

compass

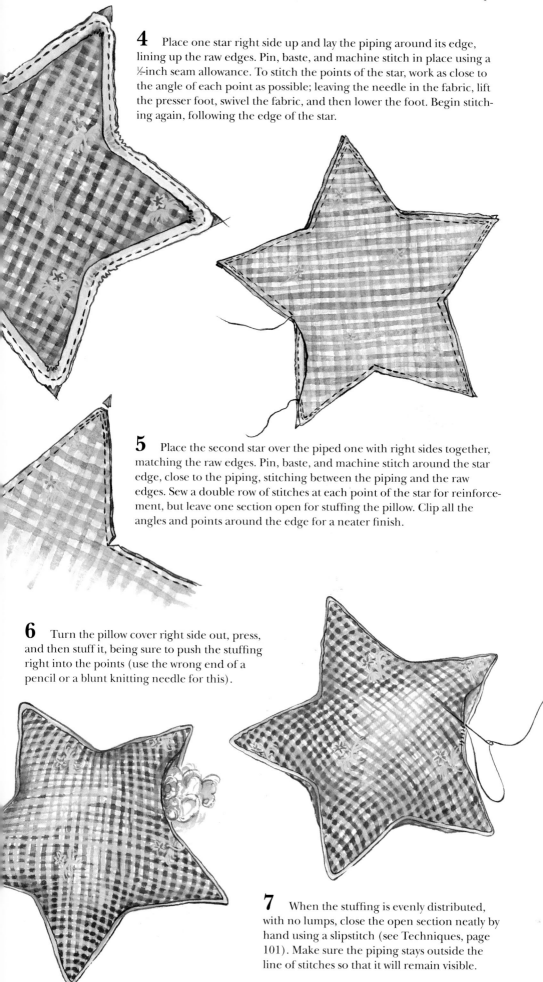

4 Place one star right side up and lay the piping around its edge, lining up the raw edges. Pin, baste, and machine stitch in place using a ½-inch seam allowance. To stitch the points of the star, work as close to the angle of each point as possible; leaving the needle in the fabric, lift the presser foot, swivel the fabric, and then lower the foot. Begin stitching again, following the edge of the star.

5 Place the second star over the piped one with right sides together, matching the raw edges. Pin, baste, and machine stitch around the star edge, close to the piping, stitching between the piping and the raw edges. Sew a double row of stitches at each point of the star for reinforcement, but leave one section open for stuffing the pillow. Clip all the angles and points around the edge for a neater finish.

6 Turn the pillow cover right side out, press, and then stuff it, being sure to push the stuffing right into the points (use the wrong end of a pencil or a blunt knitting needle for this).

7 When the stuffing is evenly distributed, with no lumps, close the open section neatly by hand using a slipstitch (see Techniques, page 101). Make sure the piping stays outside the line of stitches so that it will remain visible.

14

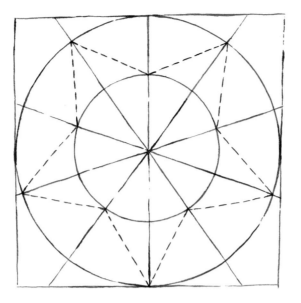

1 Make a star-shaped template on the paper by drawing a large circle with an 11½-inch radius and a second smaller one inside it with a 6½-inch radius. With a protractor and compass, mark off ten equidistant points around the outer circle, each exactly 36° apart. Using these marks and starting from the middle point, divide the square into ten sections. Use these reference points to draw an accurate five-pointed star. Cut out the star to use as a pattern.

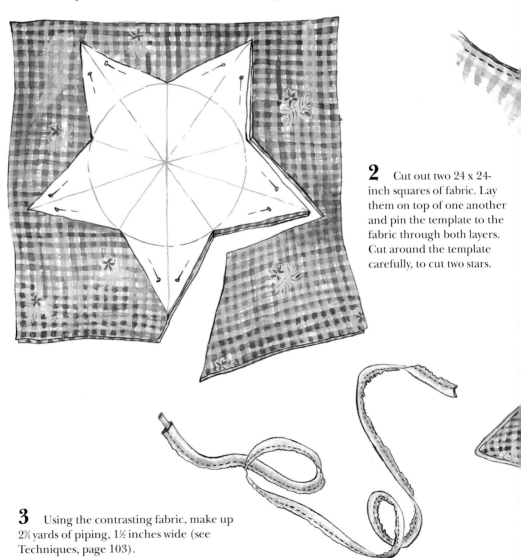

2 Cut out two 24 x 24-inch squares of fabric. Lay them on top of one another and pin the template to the fabric through both layers. Cut around the template carefully, to cut two stars.

3 Using the contrasting fabric, make up 2¾ yards of piping, 1½ inches wide (see Techniques, page 103).

bee bolster

Bolster-shaped cushions are often associated with formal Empire furniture, but the shape can be used in a variety of situations: a metal daybed can be softened with a bolster, as can a particularly upright backed sofa or a rather firm chaise-longue. The French use them as pillows on their beds, and little ones make useful neck rests. This one is made from a bee motif fabric with beautifully pleated ends, and looks very stylish on a buttoned sofa.

materials & equipment

⅝ yard embroidered bee fabric, 45 inches wide

⅝ yard solid fabric, 45 inches wide

1¼ yards thick decorative braid

¾ yard coordinating decorative braid

⅜ yard a third braid

6 x 17-inch bolster form

compass or string, pencil and pin

dressmaker's chalk

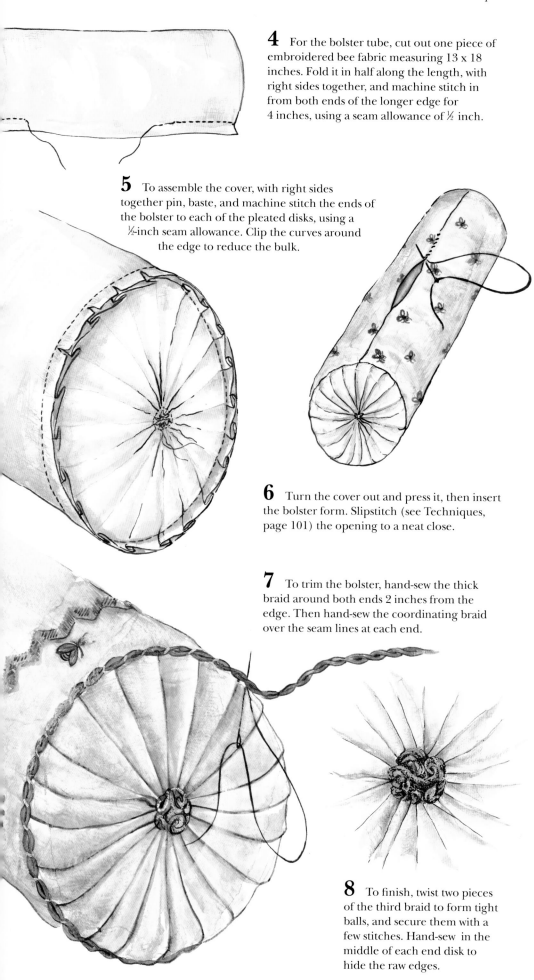

4 For the bolster tube, cut out one piece of embroidered bee fabric measuring 13 x 18 inches. Fold it in half along the length, with right sides together, and machine stitch in from both ends of the longer edge for 4 inches, using a seam allowance of ½ inch.

5 To assemble the cover, with right sides together pin, baste, and machine stitch the ends of the bolster to each of the pleated disks, using a ½-inch seam allowance. Clip the curves around the edge to reduce the bulk.

6 Turn the cover out and press it, then insert the bolster form. Slipstitch (see Techniques, page 101) the opening to a neat close.

7 To trim the bolster, hand-sew the thick braid around both ends 2 inches from the edge. Then hand-sew the coordinating braid over the seam lines at each end.

8 To finish, twist two pieces of the third braid to form tight balls, and secure them with a few stitches. Hand-sew in the middle of each end disk to hide the raw edges.

1 To make the end pieces, cut out two circles of solid fabric with a 12-inch diameter. Fold them both in half and then quarters, and mark these sections with dressmaker's chalk. Open each disk out again and draw a circle with a 5-inch diameter in its center. Fold into quarters and cut out the inner circle to form a ring.

2 Measure and mark points around the disks at alternating 1-inch and ¾-inch intervals. Tuck each ¾-inch fold under the 1-inch section and pin and baste the pleats in place, ½ inch from the edge of the outer circumference.

3 Now gather pleats around the inner ring to close the center gap and form two circles for the bolster ends. Secure the pleats tightly in position with basting stitches.

striped
tufted cushion

Looking just like a mattress in miniature and made in heavy blue and
cream cotton, this functional tufted pad is the ideal solution for
softening wooden or metal seats. Because the casing is stuffed and the
surface contours are made by hand tufting, you can make cushions of
any size to make window seats or wooden benches more comfortable.

materials & equipment

1¼ yards cotton fabric, 45 inches wide

enough stuffing to fill the 14 x 22 x 3-inch finished cover

dressmaker's chalk

heavy thread

heavy duty needle

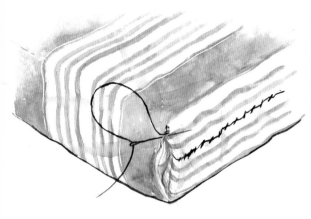

6 Tuck the ends of both pointed corners inside the body of the pillow so you have two squared-up seams and the pillow is an equal width at both ends and an equal depth all around. Slipstitch the tucks neatly closed.

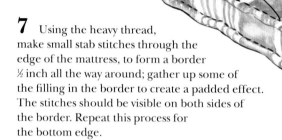

7 Using the heavy thread, make small stab stitches through the edge of the mattress, to form a border ½ inch all the way around; gather up some of the filling in the border to create a padded effect. The stitches should be visible on both sides of the border. Repeat this process for the bottom edge.

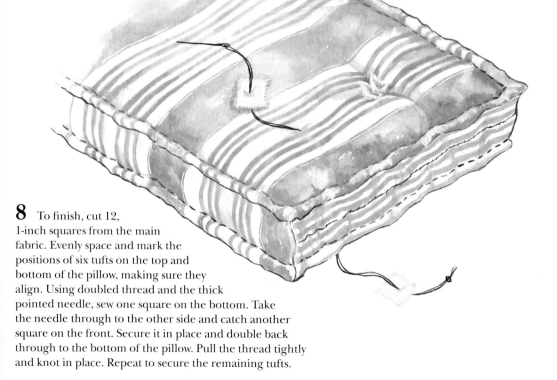

8 To finish, cut 12, 1-inch squares from the main fabric. Evenly space and mark the positions of six tufts on the top and bottom of the pillow, making sure they align. Using doubled thread and the thick pointed needle, sew one square on the bottom. Take the needle through to the other side and catch another square on the front. Secure it in place and double back through to the bottom of the pillow. Pull the thread tightly and knot in place. Repeat to secure the remaining tufts.

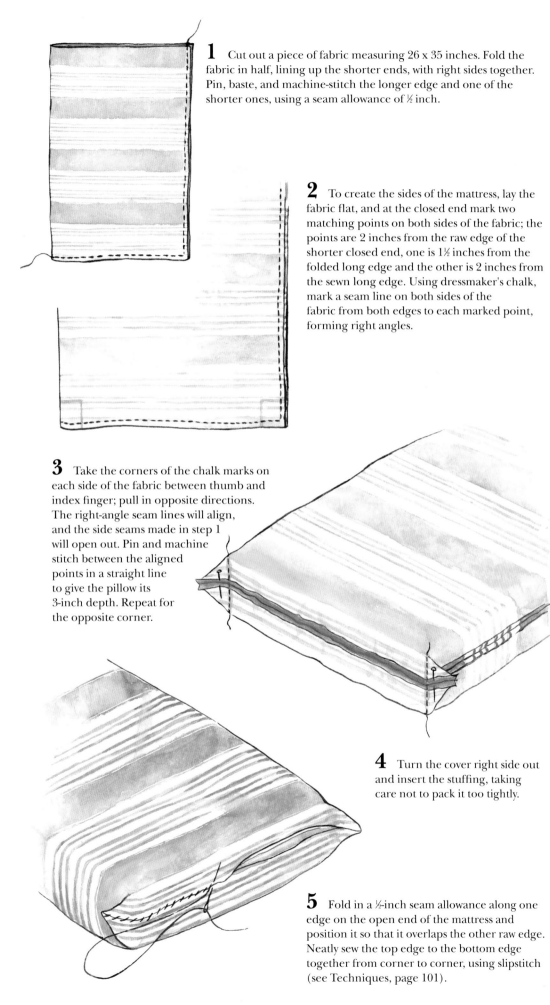

1 Cut out a piece of fabric measuring 26 x 35 inches. Fold the fabric in half, lining up the shorter ends, with right sides together. Pin, baste, and machine-stitch the longer edge and one of the shorter ones, using a seam allowance of ½ inch.

2 To create the sides of the mattress, lay the fabric flat, and at the closed end mark two matching points on both sides of the fabric; the points are 2 inches from the raw edge of the shorter closed end, one is 1½ inches from the folded long edge and the other is 2 inches from the sewn long edge. Using dressmaker's chalk, mark a seam line on both sides of the fabric from both edges to each marked point, forming right angles.

3 Take the corners of the chalk marks on each side of the fabric between thumb and index finger; pull in opposite directions. The right-angle seam lines will align, and the side seams made in step 1 will open out. Pin and machine stitch between the aligned points in a straight line to give the pillow its 3-inch depth. Repeat for the opposite corner.

4 Turn the cover right side out and insert the stuffing, taking care not to pack it too tightly.

5 Fold in a ½-inch seam allowance along one edge on the open end of the mattress and position it so that it overlaps the other raw edge. Neatly sew the top edge to the bottom edge together from corner to corner, using slipstitch (see Techniques, page 101).

ball fringe
in the round

Circular pillow forms are readily available, though they tend to be of the pancake variety. This pill-shaped size can lend itself to both traditional or modern looks. Here a creamy dotted Swiss looks almost ethereal with the addition of two rows of cotton bobble fringe. This looks simpler to make than it is, so follow the steps carefully.

materials & equipment

1¼ yards dotted swiss fabric, 60 inches wide

2¼ yards piping cord

2¼ yards ball fringe

15-inch round pillow form, 4 inches deep

contrasting-colored basting thread

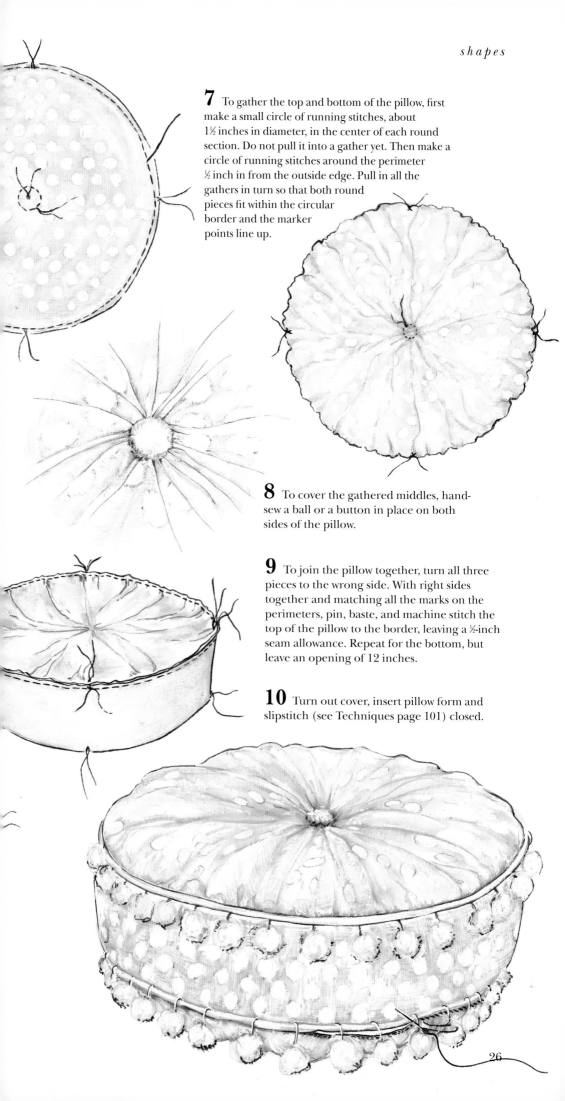

7 To gather the top and bottom of the pillow, first make a small circle of running stitches, about 1½ inches in diameter, in the center of each round section. Do not pull it into a gather yet. Then make a circle of running stitches around the perimeter ½ inch in from the outside edge. Pull in all the gathers in turn so that both round pieces fit within the circular border and the marker points line up.

8 To cover the gathered middles, hand-sew a ball or a button in place on both sides of the pillow.

9 To join the pillow together, turn all three pieces to the wrong side. With right sides together and matching all the marks on the perimeters, pin, baste, and machine stitch the top of the pillow to the border, leaving a ½-inch seam allowance. Repeat for the bottom, but leave an opening of 12 inches.

10 Turn out cover, insert pillow form and slipstitch (see Techniques page 101) closed.

1 For the top and bottom of the pillow cut out two circles of fabric, each with an 18-inch diameter. For the side panel cut out a strip measuring 5 x 49 inches.

2 Place the side strip right side up. Cut the length of fringe in half and pin and baste a length of bobble fringe along each of the outside edges of the side strip, matching the raw edges.

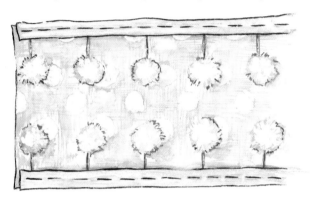

3 Next make the piping by cutting out the two lengths of fabric on the bias (see Techniques, page 103), each measuring 1 x 49 inches. Make two lengths of piping (see Techniques, page 103).

4 Lay the piping over the bobble fringe so that the raw edges of the piping point away from the balls, which should lie toward the middle of the side strip. Pin, baste, and machine stitch through all three layers. Repeat for the other long edge of the side strip.

5 To join the ends of the side strip, place the short ends right sides together and machine stitch with a ½-inch seam allowance. Press the seam open. This completes the circular border.

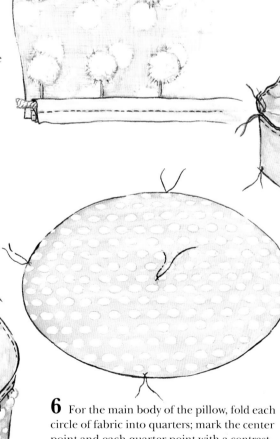

6 For the main body of the pillow, fold each circle of fabric into quarters; mark the center point and each quarter point with a contrasting-colored stitch, on both the perimeters. Use the stitched markers around the two perimeters to mark quarter points on both the top and bottom edges of the circular border.

above left A white woolen bobble and fan edging trims a strong animal print in beige and red woven cotton.
above center An exquisitely delicate cut velvet and chenille tassel in rich shades of purple and gold dangles on the corner of a woven organdy ribbon cushion.
above right The harlequin pattern of this fabric emphasizes the long bolster shape. The edges are trimmed with cotton tasseled fringe.
right This very impressive-looking pillow is made from burgundy velvet. The regal-looking crest is embroidered directly onto the front and set off beautifully by the rich gold metallic piping, twisted at the corners.

above Gaufraged golden thistles on a wine-colored velvet, edged in two-tone rope and tassels.
left A patchwork of rich and sumptuous silks, separated by a golden metallic ribbon, edged in a multicolored tasseled fringe.
below left A cotton and gaufraged velvet stripe looks smart with chenille fringing.
below center Rich woven damask needs only the adornment of a thin rope border.
below right Jewel-colored wool and mohair to keep you warm.

use of fabrics

Fabric is available in a bewildering array. However, if you think beyond the three basic elements of any fabric – color, pattern, and texture – you will see that there are all sorts of ways you can play with these elements for decorative effect. By piecing together clever contrasts and combinations of fabrics you can achieve spectacular results.

top of page A lush harlequin velvet pillow with novel tassels sits atop a knife-edged golden cotton damask one.
above Antique needlepoint pillows are very popular, and harder and harder to find. This lovely old one is trimmed with golden ribbon and a tasseled fringe.
left Variations on a color theme: burgundy and grass green in different fabrics – above inexpensive display felt, and below, rough burlap.

stripes into squares

A pillow to add a touch of imperial style to a daybed or sofa.
Link the material and tassel to other color themes in the room, or
perhaps let it stand alone to make a bold statement in what might
otherwise be a drab corner. Here, construction and design
rely on four triangles mitered together into a square.

materials & equipment

1½ yards striped cotton, 45 inches wide

¾ yard thick piping cord for ties

decorative tassel

18-inch square pillow form

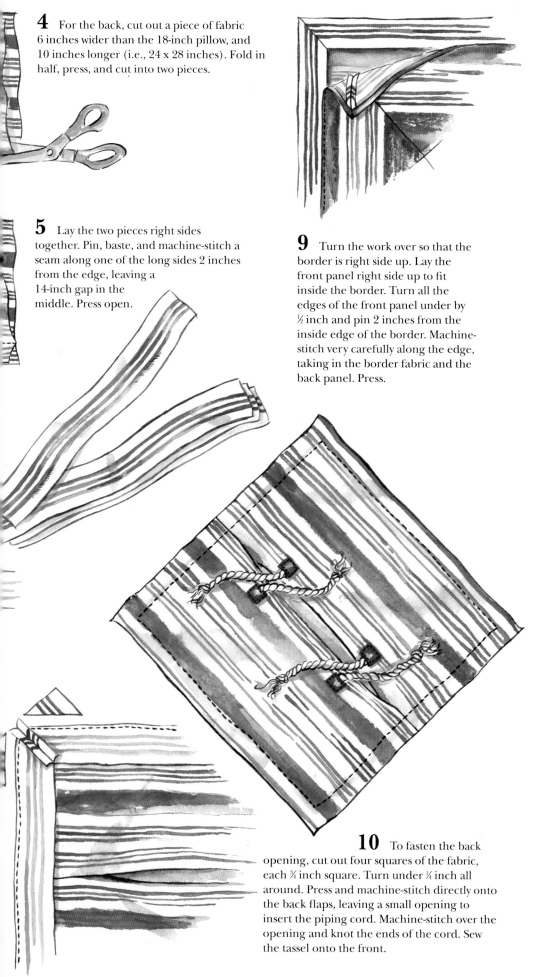

4 For the back, cut out a piece of fabric 6 inches wider than the 18-inch pillow, and 10 inches longer (i.e., 24 x 28 inches). Fold in half, press, and cut into two pieces.

5 Lay the two pieces right sides together. Pin, baste, and machine-stitch a seam along one of the long sides 2 inches from the edge, leaving a 14-inch gap in the middle. Press open.

9 Turn the work over so that the border is right side up. Lay the front panel right side up to fit inside the border. Turn all the edges of the front panel under by ½ inch and pin 2 inches from the inside edge of the border. Machine-stitch very carefully along the edge, taking in the border fabric and the back panel. Press.

10 To fasten the back opening, cut out four squares of the fabric, each ¾ inch square. Turn under ¼ inch all around. Press and machine-stitch directly onto the back flaps, leaving a small opening to insert the piping cord. Machine-stitch over the opening and knot the ends of the cord. Sew the tassel onto the front.

32

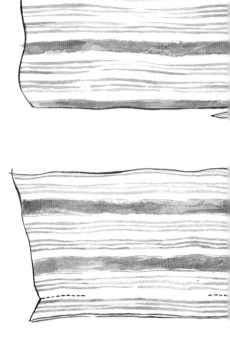

1 For the front of the pillow, cut out four pieces of fabric into identical triangles, each 18½ x 13¼ x 13¼ inches, which includes a ½-inch seam allowance.

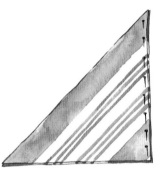

2 Place two of the triangles right sides together. Carefully align the stripes and pin, baste, and machine-stitch along a ½-inch seam. Repeat for the other two triangles. Open out and press the seams open.

6 Cut out four rectangular strips of striped fabric, each 3 x 23 inches. Position the stripes lengthwise down each of the strips, centered on the width.

3 Place the two seamed triangles right sides together. Carefully align the stripes, and pin, baste, and machine stitch together along the straight edge. Press open the seam.

7 Place a strip, face down, along one edge of the right side of the back panel. Lay the next strip against an adjoining edge, fold back the corners, miter and press. Pin and machine stitch the mitered edges. Cut off the surplus fabric, leaving a ½-inch seam allowance. Repeat for all four corners and press seams open.

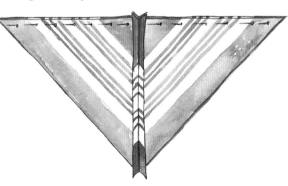

8 Lay the mitered border wrong side up over the right side of the back panel. Pin a machine-stitch along the outer edge, leavi a ½-inch seam allowance. Turn the border right side out and press.

ribbon weave

This sumptuous woven ribbon pillow works on the simple principle of basket weaving. Seven different shades of velvet ribbon are cut into strips of equal length and woven across the surface of the pillow. This idea can be adapted using just two or three colors for a checkerboard effect or even just one color to show off the weave. The velvet tassels on the corners add the perfect finishing touch.

materials & equipment

⅝ yard thin interlining fabric

⅝ yard velvet fabric, 45 inches wide

*seven different colors of velvet ribbon, 1 inch wide,
with a total length of 21 yards*

2¼ yards velvet cording

four tassels

18-inch zipper

18-inch square pillow form

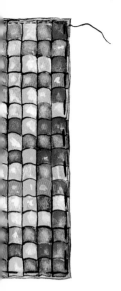

7 Lay the velvet cording around the edge of the back piece on the right side, lining up the raw edges. Pin and baste together.

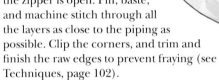

8 With right sides facing, position the front section over the corded back panel, making sure the zipper is open. Pin, baste, and machine stitch through all the layers as close to the piping as possible. Clip the corners, and trim and finish the raw edges to prevent fraying (see Techniques, page 102).

9 Turn the cover right side out, insert the pillow form and close the zipper. Attach a tassel to each corner with small hand stitches.

1 To create the ribbon effect on the front, cut 19-inch strips from each color of ribbon. It does not matter if there are more strips of some colors – this will add to the effect. Cut out a piece of interlining fabric 19 inches square.

2 Pin the strips face up along one edge of the interlining, leaving a ½-inch gap on each of the sides. Try to achieve a random effect when positioning the colors. Baste, and machine stitch along the top of the ribbons to secure them, allowing a ½-inch seam allowance.

4 Continue weaving the ribbons until the interlining is covered, and then baste the three loose sides down.

3 Starting from the top, weave the remaining ribbons horizontally, threading them under and over the vertical ribbons. Alternate the colors to create a random pattern and anchor them at the sides with pins. Push each ribbon tightly against the one above.

5 For the back, cut out two pieces of velvet measuring 10½ x 19 inches. Place the panels right sides together, and along one of the longer sides, machine stitch in from the edge for 2 inches on each side; use a seam allowance of 1 inch. Open the seams out and press.

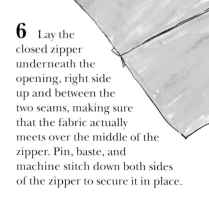

6 Lay the closed zipper underneath the opening, right side up and between the two seams, making sure that the fabric actually meets over the middle of the zipper. Pin, baste, and machine stitch down both sides of the zipper to secure it in place.

floppy-edge pillow

Stone-washed silk has an irresistible texture. Here, muted blue and purple silk are pieced together to form a striped pattern. The deep full flaps that make the border, combined with the nature of the fabric, give this pillow a wonderfully floppy and extravagant feel that will add a touch of sheer luxury to a room.

materials & equipment

1¼ yards purple stone-washed silk,
45 inches wide

⅞ yard blue stone-washed silk,
45 inches wide

18-inch square pillow form

8 Turn the completed deep border right side out and press along the fold line on each strip to form a square.

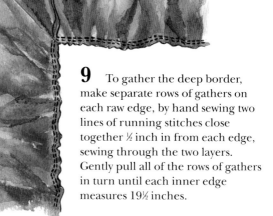

9 To gather the deep border, make separate rows of gathers on each raw edge, by hand sewing two lines of running stitches close together ½ inch in from each edge, sewing through the two layers. Gently pull all of the rows of gathers in turn until each inner edge measures 19½ inches.

10 Take the back panel and lay it flat with the right side up. Place the border over it, lining up the gathered edges of the flap with the raw edges of the back section. Pin, baste, and machine stitch in place using a ½-inch seam allowance.

11 Press the border outward, then turn the work over and press the narrow seam allowances around all four sides toward the middle.

12 With the right side up, place the front panel over the wrong side of the back panel, lining up the turned-in edges on the front with the stitching line around the edge of the back. Pin and baste the two pieces together and join them with a tight ¼-inch zigzag stitch or a topstitch. Make sure you stitch right against the edge of the front panel.

13 Press the pillow cover and insert the pillow form through the overlap at the back. Make sure the pillow form is completely covered.

1 For the back, cut out two pieces of purple silk, each measuring 12 x 19½ inches. Turn under a double ¼-inch hem along one of the longer edges on both pieces; pin, baste, and machine stitch it in place.

2 Overlap the hemmed edges of each panel by 4 inches and pin and baste along both side edges of the overlap. The back should now measure 19½ x 19½ inches with a deep flap for inserting the pillow form and closing the cover.

3 For the front, cut out two panels of purple silk, each measuring 6½ x 19½ inches and one panel of blue silk measuring 8 x 19½ inches.

4 Place the three panels side by side, matching the long edges, with the blue panel in the middle. With right sides together, pin, baste, and machine stitch the blue silk to one side of each of the purple pieces, using a seam allowance of ½ inch. Turn under a ½-inch seam allowance on all four sides and baste it in place. This is the front panel.

5 For the border flaps, cut two strips 9 x 33 inches from each color of silk fabric. Fold the strips in half down the length with the right side out and press to mark the fold line.

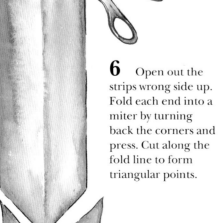

6 Open out the strips wrong side up. Fold each end into a miter by turning back the corners and press. Cut along the fold line to form triangular points.

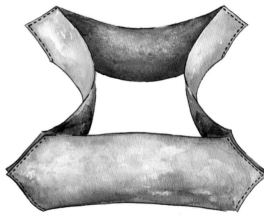

7 Place the strips corner to corner, with alternate colors touching. With right sides together, pin, baste, and machine stitch the mitered corners together using a seam allowance of ½ inch.

crazy velvet patchwork

The age-old craft of patchwork has enduring appeal. Here, a puzzle of velvet scraps, some slightly bald and worn, have been pieced together in a random fashion and the seams disguised with decorative feather stitching in a strong color. This idea would work equally well with a selection of silk scraps.

materials & equipment

assorted colors of velvet to cover the 16 x 18-inch front section

⅝ yard velvet, 45 inches wide, for the back

2¼ yards rope edging

16 x 18-inch pillow form

one sheet each of drawing paper, tracing paper, and thick paper

embroidery floss in a contrasting color

crewel needle

5 Once the front section is in one piece, sew over all the seam lines with stranded floss using feather stitch (see Techniques, page 101).

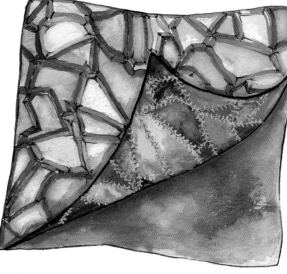

6 For the back, cut out a 17 x 19-inch piece of velvet. Finish the raw edges (see Techniques, page 102), turn a ½-inch seam allowance to the wrong side and press in place. Lay the front and back sections right sides together.

7 Neatly hand-sew the front and back sections together along three of the sides using an overcasting stitch.

8 Turn the cover right side out and insert the pillow form. Slipstitch the opening neatly, leaving a small gap to insert the end of the rope edging.

9 Cut the rope edging to fit the edge of the pillow and hand-sew it around the edges, inserting the ends of the rope into the small gap before sewing it closed for a neat finish.

44

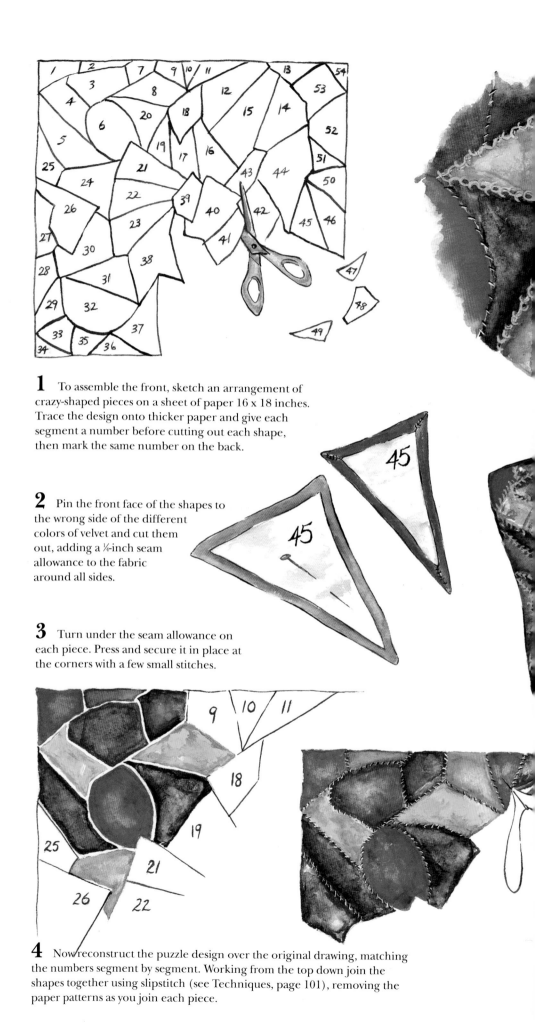

1 To assemble the front, sketch an arrangement of crazy-shaped pieces on a sheet of paper 16 x 18 inches. Trace the design onto thicker paper and give each segment a number before cutting out each shape, then mark the same number on the back.

2 Pin the front face of the shapes to the wrong side of the different colors of velvet and cut them out, adding a ¼-inch seam allowance to the fabric around all sides.

3 Turn under the seam allowance on each piece. Press and secure it in place at the corners with a few small stitches.

4 Now reconstruct the puzzle design over the original drawing, matching the numbers segment by segment. Working from the top down join the shapes together using slipstitch (see Techniques, page 101), removing the paper patterns as you join each piece.

left These soft and comfy fleece pillows have been blanket-stitched around the edges in contrasting colors.

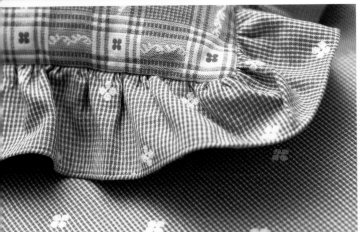

above A fresh country weave has a coordinating, lightly gathered ruffle, used as a single layer with a tiny hem.
top right A deep quilted border has been stitched with heavy linen thread on plain red linen fabric.

center right Antique striped linen has been mitered to form a square pattern, with a red piping border.
right A white cotton triangle has a tightly ruffled border of wired burlap ribbon in contrasting khaki.

opposite page, top from left A linen damask pillow has an outer casing of the finest silk organza with a deeply ruffled edge – the ultimate luxury; a thin, inexpensive plain linen pillow with a ruffled edge, outlined in the palest blue bias binding; twisted rope borders a stylish tailored linen stripe.

borders & edgings

By emphasizing the outline of a pillow you can turn a bland accessory that fades into the background into something that really gets noticed. Borders come in all shapes and forms – from the subtlest piping to more dramatic ruffles or flaps, edgings are integral to the design.

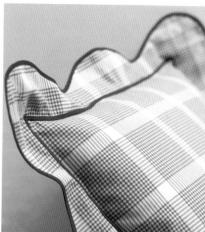

above Two pillows made from antique woven linen: one has a pillowcase flap with covered buttons for closure; the other has a deeper top closing flap, which uses the same fabric at right angles, and hand-stitched buttonholes.

top right An elegant wavy flap is edged in narrow bias binding in a contrasting red to provide a tailored finish that emphasizes the curves.

center right Linen dishtowels come out of the kitchen to make excellent pillows, their borders providing a natural flap to stitch around.

right A double gathered border is made from strips of plain red fabric, gathering onto a thick piping cord.

scallops
and zigzags

There is a timeless magic in scallops and zigzags, well-known decorative devices for fabrics. These natural linens in neutral beige and white look fresh and modern, and can be applied to most shapes and sizes to great effect. The instructions here are for scallops, but the same technique can be used to create a pointed border like the one below.

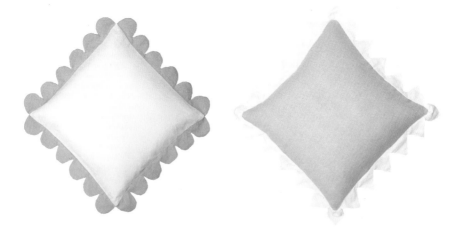

materials & equipment

⅝ yard beige linen, 45 inches wide

⅝ yard white linen, 45 inches wide

18-inch square pillow form

compass or circular object

ruler

8 Machine stitch the open hemmed seam allowance on one side to the main body of the same piece on the right side of the fabric, starting 3 inches in from each side and 1¼ inches above the central fold.

9 Now press the back panel with both seam allowances pointing toward the piece just stitched.

10 Lay the back panel right side up and stitch two narrow parallel rows of vertical stitching extending for 1¼ inches from the central fold and beginning 3 inches from the sides, thus securing the flap.

11 To make the ties, cut two strips of white linen fabric measuring ¾ x 12 inches. Neatly hem the long sides of each strip, and press. Attach one tie to the middle of each side of the back opening by machine stitching across its width 1¼ inches from the central fold. Finish the ends of both the ties by cutting them on the diagonal.

12 Next place the four scalloped borders along each edge of the right side of the front piece, lining up the raw edges and leaving a ½-inch gap at each end. Pin, baste, and machine stitch down each side.

13 Place the finished back piece over the front piece, right sides facing. Pin, baste, and machine stitch the front to the back with a ½-inch seam allowance, being careful to stitch just *inside* the seam attaching the scallops to the front piece. Finish the raw edges (see Techniques, page 102) and clip the corners. Turn the casing right side out through the flap. Press then insert the pillow form and fasten the ties.

1 To make the scallops, cut out four strips of beige fabric, each 7 x 19 inches. Fold them in half lengthwise with right sides together and press.

2 Using a circular object or a compass, draw six circles on the strip, each with a 2½-inch diameter.
Position the line of circles so there is a ½-inch gap at each open end, a ⅜-inch gap in between each circle, and a 1-inch gap between the bottom of each circle and the raw edge. Draw a straight line through the middle of all six circles. To create the scallops, follow the outline of the top half of each circle and extend the outline ¼ inch below the straight line, linking the half circles together.

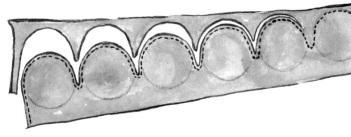

3 Machine stitch along the line of scallops on all four strips and cut out.

4 Trim the edges to ¼ inch and snip between the scallops. Turn right side out, pushing the scallops into shape, and press.

5 For the front of the pillow cut out a piece of white fabric measuring 19 inches square. For the back, cut out two pieces of white fabric, each measuring 11½ x 19 inches.

6 To make the back, both pieces right sides together. Machine stitch 3 inches in from each side along the longer edge, with a 2-inch seam allowance.

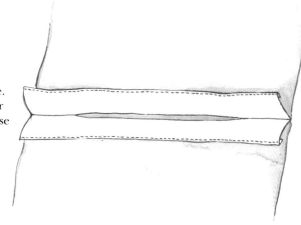

7 Turn the back panel wrong side up and open out the seam allowance. On each seam allowance, turn under ½ inch and machine stitch a hem close to the raw edge.

box-pleated border

Box pleats make a stylish edging for a tailored pillow. Although they take quite a bit of fabric, they are simple to make and very effective. Stripes lend themselves particularly well to this technique, though care needs to be taken to keep them in line. On this pillow, the narrow stripe appears only on the front of the pleats.

materials & equipment

⅜ yard cotton motif main fabric, 45 inches wide

⅝ yard cotton fabric (this one features alternate panels of 3½-inch-wide stripes)

10 x 16-inch pillow form

5 Snip into the raw edges of the fabric almost as far as the seam allowance on the corner pleats.

Lay the front panel right side up. Place the border over it with the large box pleats facing down (the striped ones in this case). Match the corners and line up the raw edges, then pin and baste the border to the panel, using a ½-inch seam allowance.

6 Now place the back panel over the bordered front piece, right side down and lining up the four sides. Pin, baste, and machine-stitch around three sides of the cover and turn it right side out.

7 Insert the pillow form and slipstitch (see Techniques, page 101) the opening on the back to a neat close.

54

1 Cut two pieces 11 x 17 inches from the main fabric, with a motif centered on one piece. For the border, cut out a 7 x 113-inch strip from the striped fabric, joining lengths where needed.

2 Stitch the short ends of the border strip together with right sides facing and stripes matching, then press the seam open. Fold the completed circle in half lengthwise with wrong sides together and press the fold line.

3 To make a box pleat, fold the fabric about 1 inch into itself on both sides; if your fabric is striped like this one try to keep the pattern the same on each boxed section. Pin the pleat in place on the raw edge and repeat all the way along the strip. Baste the pleats in position and press.

4 Lay the border out to make a rectangle with an even number of box pleats on each side; here there are five boxes on the top and bottom and three boxes on each side.

53

double ruffle taffeta

Taffeta has a luxurious quality, and there is no better way to see it than when it is gathered and bunched. Here a tiny check is used with a double ruffle effect. The outside ruffle is a single layer of fabric, and the smaller inside one uses the fabric doubled and tightly gathered, to make an especially sumptuous pillow.

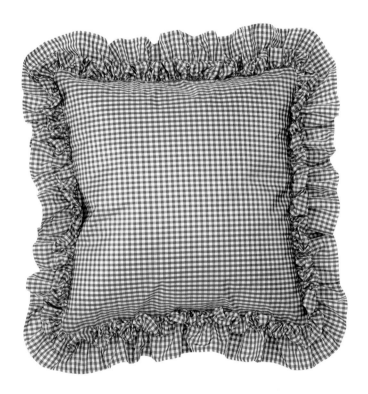

materials & equipment

1¼ yards taffeta, 45 inches wide

18-inch square pillow form

15-inch zipper

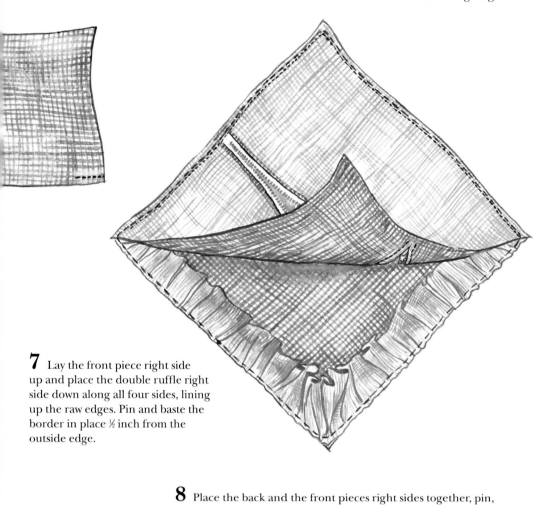

7 Lay the front piece right side up and place the double ruffle right side down along all four sides, lining up the raw edges. Pin and baste the border in place ½ inch from the outside edge.

8 Place the back and the front pieces right sides together, pin, baste, and machine stitch all around the edge with a ½-inch seam allowance. Stitch *inside* the gathering stitches. At each corner work the stitches in a curve, not a sharp right angle. Trim the edges and clip the corners. Turn the cover out through the open zipper and insert the pillow form.

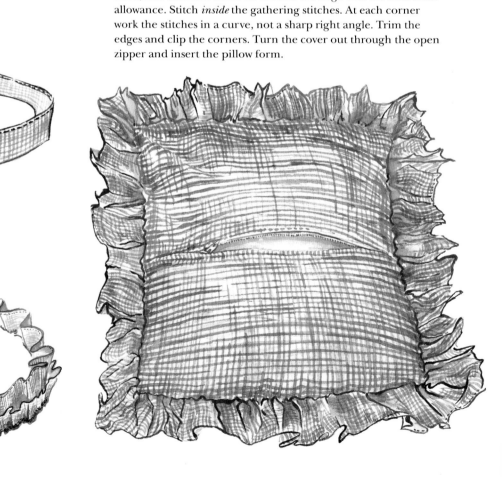

1 For the front section, cut out one piece of fabric measuring 19 x 19 inches. For the back, cut out two panels of fabric measuring 10½ x 19 inches. For the ruffle, cut out two strips, each measuring 4 x 160 inches, joining lengths where necessary.

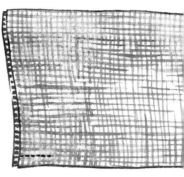

2 To make the back, place the two panels right sides together, and along one of the longer sides machine stitch for 2 inches in from the edge on each side, leaving a seam allowance of 1 inch. Open the seams out and press.

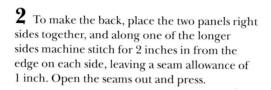

3 Turn the back panel over to the right side and lay the closed zipper underneath the opening, right side up and between the two seams, making sure that the fabric actually meets over the middle of the zipper. Pin, baste, and machine stitch down each side of the zipper, using a zipper foot if you have one. Make sure the zipper is *open* before you continue sewing.

4 To make the border, with right sides together stitch the short ends of one of the ruffle strips to form one piece. Repeat for the other strip and press the seams open. Neatly hem one of the strips by turning in ¼ inch on one long edge, and machine stitch all the way around.

5 Fold the other strip in half, wrong sides together, but do not press the fold. Place the folded strip alongside the right side of the hemmed one and line up the raw edges, then baste all the way around ½ inch from the edge.

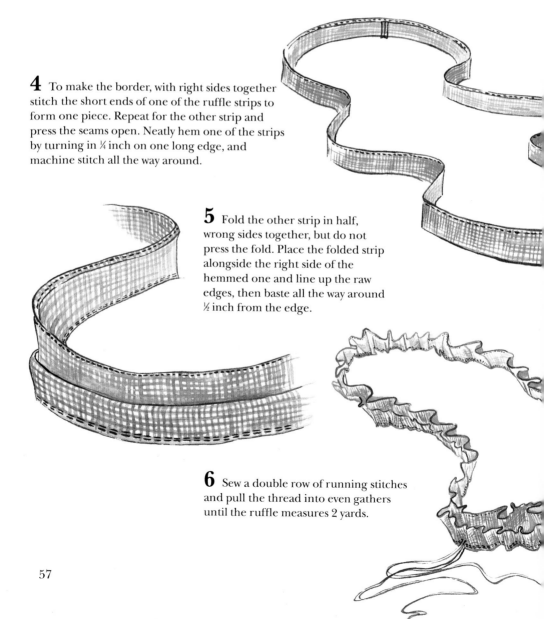

6 Sew a double row of running stitches and pull the thread into even gathers until the ruffle measures 2 yards.

double-flanged border

Two sophisticated woven silk patterns look very stylish with double flaps that give a glimpse of the contrasting fabric. The thinness of the silk lends itself particularly well to this style, which is simple to work as well in a stronger pattern. Deceptively easy to make, this pillow looks lovely in a sophisticated setting.

materials & equipment

⅞ yard figured silk, 60 inches wide

⅞ yard plain silk, 60 inches wide

18-inch square pillow form

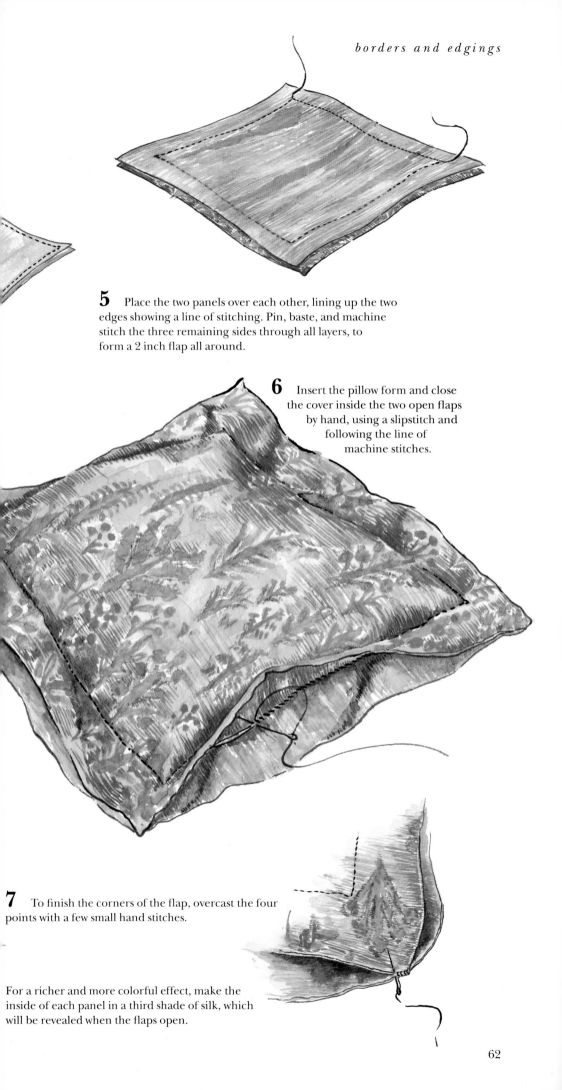

5 Place the two panels over each other, lining up the two edges showing a line of stitching. Pin, baste, and machine stitch the three remaining sides through all layers, to form a 2 inch flap all around.

6 Insert the pillow form and close the cover inside the two open flaps by hand, using a slipstitch and following the line of machine stitches.

7 To finish the corners of the flap, overcast the four points with a few small hand stitches.

For a richer and more colorful effect, make the inside of each panel in a third shade of silk, which will be revealed when the flaps open.

1 Cut four pieces of silk measuring 24 x 24 inches, two each from both fabrics. Make sure the grain runs straight and not diagonally, and that the pattern falls neatly.

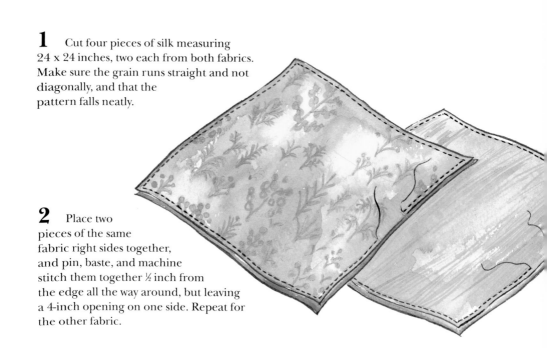

2 Place two pieces of the same fabric right sides together, and pin, baste, and machine stitch them together ½ inch from the edge all the way around, but leaving a 4-inch opening on one side. Repeat for the other fabric.

3 Turn the fabric right side out and slipstitch (see Techniques, page 101) the opening to a neat close. Press. Repeat this process for the other piece of silk.

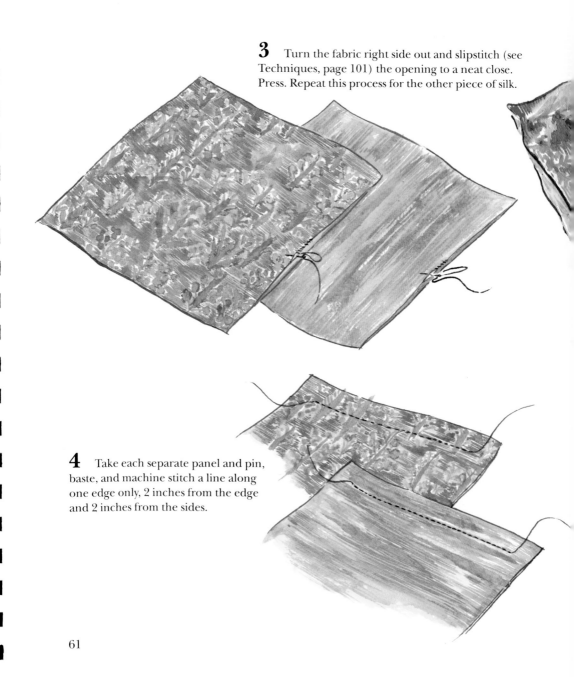

4 Take each separate panel and pin, baste, and machine stitch a line along one edge only, 2 inches from the edge and 2 inches from the sides.

right A finely woven pure white linen pillow has a surface-applied fringe made of natural hemp-like string. *below* Three rows of a deep natural cotton fringe cover the surface of white cotton to make a funky pillow.

trimmings and fastenings

Unadorned, a pillow tends to blend into the seating or surface it is placed upon. To make a feature of the pillow itself calls for some clever ideas to dress up the basic shape. Choose from the wealth of decorative trimmings and fastenings available to embellish pillows in dozens of ways.

above Three examples of back fastening ties: finished with knots; secured by square tabs of the fabric; doubled cotton with zigzagged edges. *far left* A striped silk pillow has a double-ruffled edge, with a pleated satin ribbon. *left* For a neat finish on this plaid pillow, the fan edging has been box-pleated at the corners.

left top A crewelwork pillow is trimmed in dark green linen fringe.
left below The diamond shape and the oval patch-work detail are outlined by rows of tiny bobble fringe in dark purple.

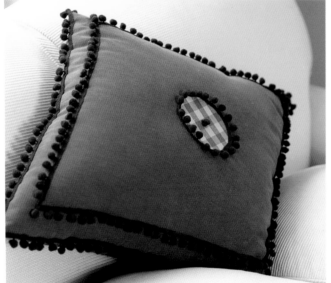

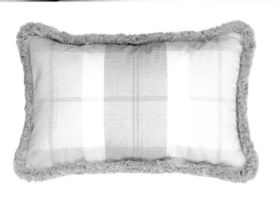

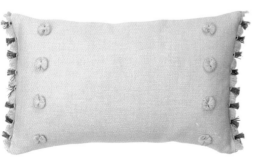

above Buttons and tufts: silk looped button; deep tufted linen; a wonderful antique handsewn button; a tuft made from cutting a square piece of fabric with pinking shears.
left Two rectangles: one has a natural ruched fringe to contrast with the subtle plaid, the other is finished in a two-tone fan edging with four tufted linen buttons sewn down each side.

65

rope-edged knotted pillow

A cool Indian madras cotton is paired with a bright red rope border, sewn directly onto the edge of the pillow. The extended corners are long enough to be knotted, for a fresh and different look. A pile of pillows in inexpensive contrasting fabrics can look gloriously exuberant.

materials & equipment

2¼ yards cotton fabric, 45 inches wide

5½ yards rope edging

18-inch square pillow form

40-inch square piece of pattern paper

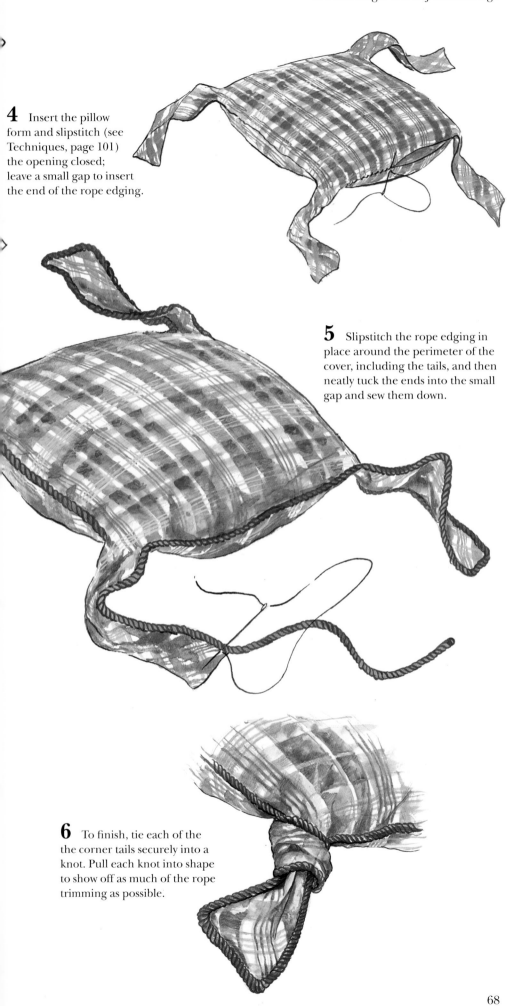

4 Insert the pillow form and slipstitch (see Techniques, page 101) the opening closed; leave a small gap to insert the end of the rope edging.

5 Slipstitch the rope edging in place around the perimeter of the cover, including the tails, and then neatly tuck the ends into the small gap and sew them down.

6 To finish, tie each of the the corner tails securely into a knot. Pull each knot into shape to show off as much of the rope trimming as possible.

1 Make a paper pattern in the shape of the template shown; the main panel of the pillow measures 19 inches square, and at each corner there is an extension or "tail" 10 inches long and 3 inches wide.

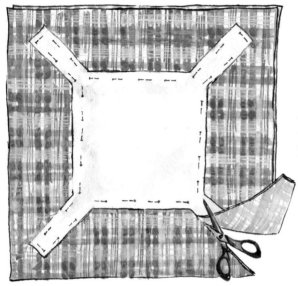

2 Fold the fabric in half, right sides together, matching raw edges. Place the paper pattern on the fabric and pin it in place. Cut out two pieces.

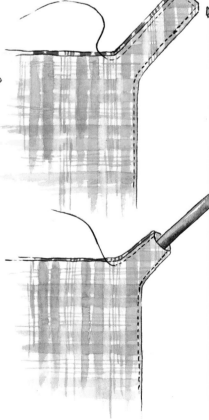

3 Remove the paper pattern and pin, baste, and machine-stitch all around the edge of the panel and the tails using a ½-inch seam allowance. Leave one side of the panel open to insert the pillow. Trim the corners and turn the tails inside out as you sew, pushing out the corners with the blunt end of a pencil or a knitting needle.

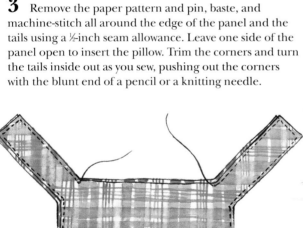

fastened
with tassels

In this formal design, pure white linen encases a silk inner lining to create a sleek and sophisticated pillow. These luxurious fabrics are appropriately dressed up with a pair of silk tassels that provide an elegant means of fastening, and the open end of the linen casing is delicately edged with drawn-thread embroidery.

materials & equipment

⅝ yard cream evenweave linen, 45 inches wide

1 yard striped silk, 45 inches wide,

two silk tassels

16-inch square pillow form

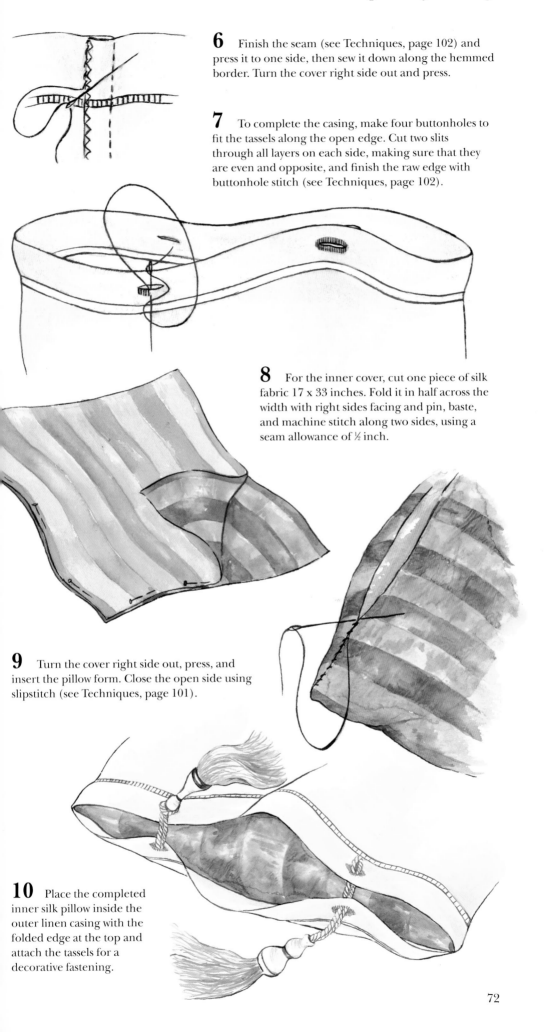

6 Finish the seam (see Techniques, page 102) and press it to one side, then sew it down along the hemmed border. Turn the cover right side out and press.

7 To complete the casing, make four buttonholes to fit the tassels along the open edge. Cut two slits through all layers on each side, making sure that they are even and opposite, and finish the raw edge with buttonhole stitch (see Techniques, page 102).

8 For the inner cover, cut one piece of silk fabric 17 x 33 inches. Fold it in half across the width with right sides facing and pin, baste, and machine stitch along two sides, using a seam allowance of ½ inch.

9 Turn the cover right side out, press, and insert the pillow form. Close the open side using slipstitch (see Techniques, page 101).

10 Place the completed inner silk pillow inside the outer linen casing with the folded edge at the top and attach the tassels for a decorative fastening.

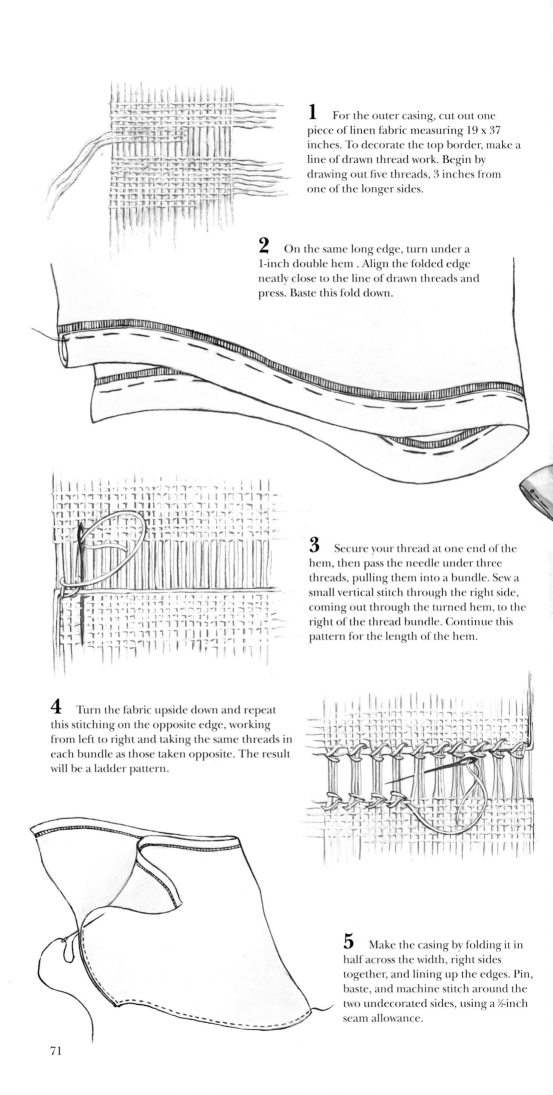

1 For the outer casing, cut out one piece of linen fabric measuring 19 x 37 inches. To decorate the top border, make a line of drawn thread work. Begin by drawing out five threads, 3 inches from one of the longer sides.

2 On the same long edge, turn under a 1-inch double hem . Align the folded edge neatly close to the line of drawn threads and press. Baste this fold down.

3 Secure your thread at one end of the hem, then pass the needle under three threads, pulling them into a bundle. Sew a small vertical stitch through the right side, coming out through the turned hem, to the right of the thread bundle. Continue this pattern for the length of the hem.

4 Turn the fabric upside down and repeat this stitching on the opposite edge, working from left to right and taking the same threads in each bundle as those taken opposite. The result will be a ladder pattern.

5 Make the casing by folding it in half across the width, right sides together, and lining up the edges. Pin, baste, and machine stitch around the two undecorated sides, using a ½-inch seam allowance.

the envelope pillow

Tassels offer a quick and easy way to add a touch of style, and they are available ready-made in all shapes and textures - from coarse rope to softest silk. Here, a neutral linen is trimmed with piping, and a burlap tassel appears to close the "envelope" flap for a pillow with a simple, understated elegance.

materials & equipment

1¼ yards linen fabric, 45 inches wide

3⅝ yards piping cord

one button

one tassel with a looped fastening

18-inch square pillow form

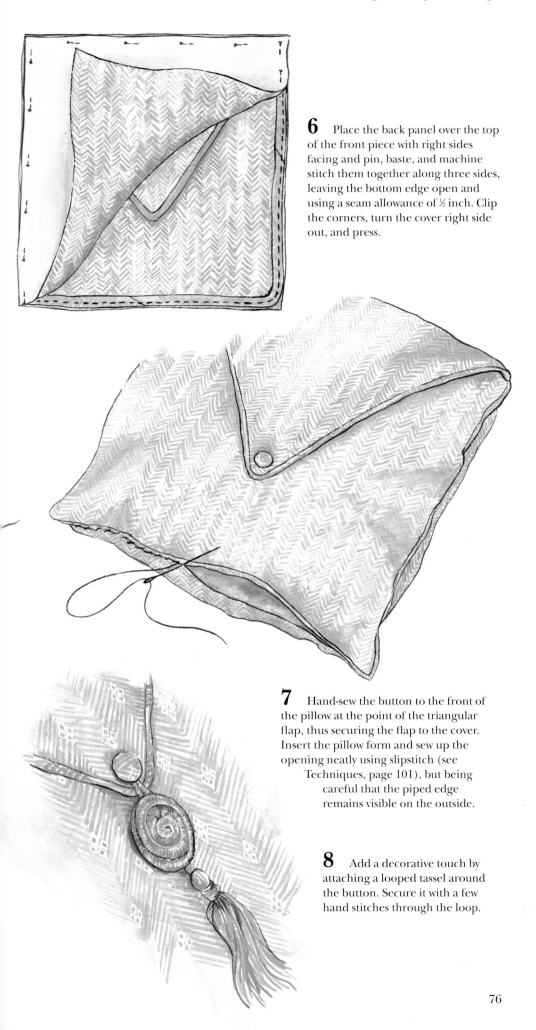

6 Place the back panel over the top of the front piece with right sides facing and pin, baste, and machine stitch them together along three sides, leaving the bottom edge open and using a seam allowance of ½ inch. Clip the corners, turn the cover right side out, and press.

7 Hand-sew the button to the front of the pillow at the point of the triangular flap, thus securing the flap to the cover. Insert the pillow form and sew up the opening neatly using slipstitch (see Techniques, page 101), but being careful that the piped edge remains visible on the outside.

8 Add a decorative touch by attaching a looped tassel around the button. Secure it with a few hand stitches through the loop.

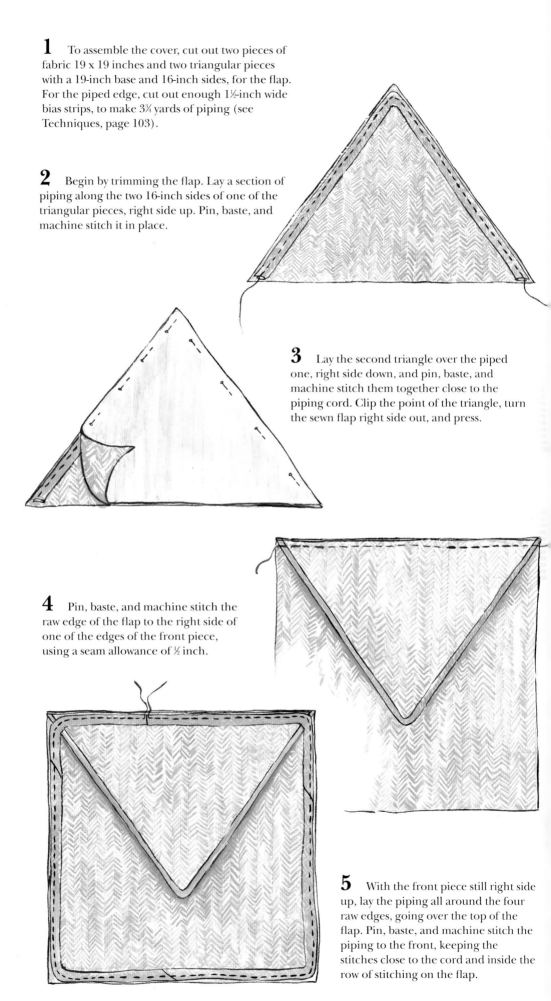

1   To assemble the cover, cut out two pieces of fabric 19 x 19 inches and two triangular pieces with a 19-inch base and 16-inch sides, for the flap. For the piped edge, cut out enough 1½-inch wide bias strips, to make 3¾ yards of piping (see Techniques, page 103).

2   Begin by trimming the flap. Lay a section of piping along the two 16-inch sides of one of the triangular pieces, right side up. Pin, baste, and machine stitch it in place.

3   Lay the second triangle over the piped one, right side down, and pin, baste, and machine stitch them together close to the piping cord. Clip the point of the triangle, turn the sewn flap right side out, and press.

4   Pin, baste, and machine stitch the raw edge of the flap to the right side of one of the edges of the front piece, using a seam allowance of ½ inch.

5   With the front piece still right side up, lay the piping all around the four raw edges, going over the top of the flap. Pin, baste, and machine stitch the piping to the front, keeping the stitches close to the cord and inside the row of stitching on the flap.

all trimmed

Rich colors and textures contrast to make a very sumptuous
pillow. Spinach-green linen forms the basis of the design with a
wide flap edged in thin red velvet piping on the outside and rich
red wool fringe on the inside. The Tyrolean floral trimming has
been sewn onto a wide cotton binding to show up the colors better.
This design lends itself to a variety of different combinations of
colors and trimmings.

materials & equipment

1⅛ yards heavyweight spinach-green linen, 45 inches wide

2¼ yards burgundy fringe

3 yards narrow bright red velvet piping

2 yards red fabric tape, 1 inch wide

2 yards decorative braid

two green buttons to match main fabric

18-inch square pillow form

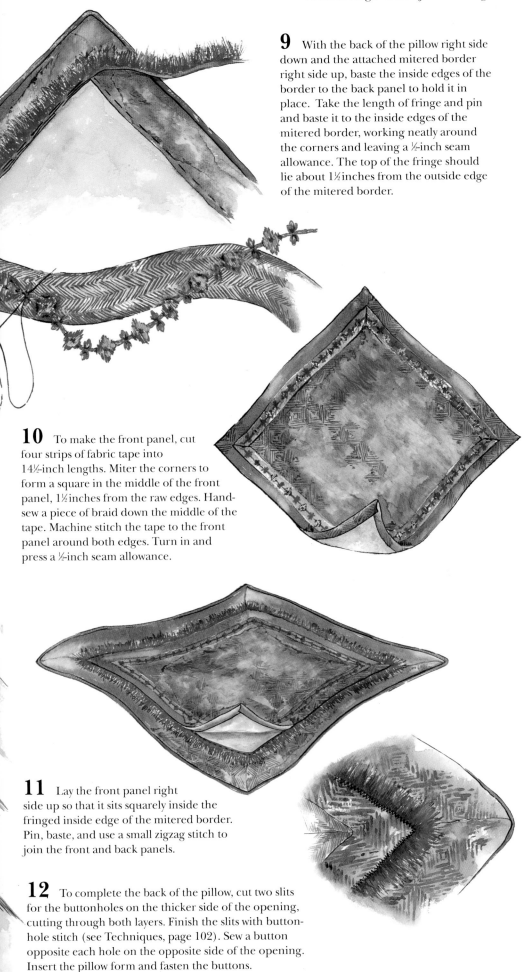

9 With the back of the pillow right side down and the attached mitered border right side up, baste the inside edges of the border to the back panel to hold it in place. Take the length of fringe and pin and baste it to the inside edges of the mitered border, working neatly around the corners and leaving a ½-inch seam allowance. The top of the fringe should lie about 1⅛ inches from the outside edge of the mitered border.

10 To make the front panel, cut four strips of fabric tape into 14½-inch lengths. Miter the corners to form a square in the middle of the front panel, 1½ inches from the raw edges. Hand-sew a piece of braid down the middle of the tape. Machine stitch the tape to the front panel around both edges. Turn in and press a ½-inch seam allowance.

11 Lay the front panel right side up so that it sits squarely inside the fringed inside edge of the mitered border. Pin, baste, and use a small zigzag stitch to join the front and back panels.

12 To complete the back of the pillow, cut two slits for the buttonholes on the thicker side of the opening, cutting through both layers. Finish the slits with buttonhole stitch (see Techniques, page 102). Sew a button opposite each hole on the opposite side of the opening. Insert the pillow form and fasten the buttons.

1 For the front, cut out one piece of main fabric measuring 19 x 19 inches. For the back, cut out two pieces of main fabric, each measuring 12½ x 23 inches. For the wide border, cut out four pieces of main fabric, each measuring 3 x 23 inches.

2 To make the back, finish both the long edges of both back panels to prevent fraying (see Techniques, page 102).

3 Lay the two back panels right sides together and pin, baste, and machine stitch a line 3½ inches in from the shorter side edges and 1 inch above one of the long edges. Then turn the fabric 90° and continue sewing a vertical line down to the same finished edge.

4 Open out the back panel and press the two seam allowances in the same direction.

5 For the border, take one strip and place it right side down along one edge of the back panel. Fold the corner of the strip in at a 45° angle. Lay the next strip, fold the corner into a miter, and press. Repeat so that all four strips are neatly mitered.

6 Remove the strips and machine stitch along each pressed fold to join the strips into a border. Trim off the excess fabric to a ½-inch seam allowance.

7 Now attach the piping to the prepared back panel. Lay the back panel flat, right side up. Pin and baste the velvet piping around the edge of the back panel, matching the raw edges and leaving a ½-inch seam allowance all around.

8 Lay the mitered border over the back panel (with piping now attached) right sides together. Pin, baste, and machine stitch together, working the stitches between the piping and the raw edges, leaving a ½-inch seam allowance. Turn right side out and press.

checked linen with contrast ties

Here, a generous beige linen flap tucks deep inside the outer checked casing, completely hiding the inner pad. Almost a slipcover in effect, and practical for slipping off for cleaning, it closes by means of two pairs of wide ties. The idea works equally effectively using the checked fabric as the inner flap and ties.

materials & equipment

⅝ yard checked linen, 45 inches wide

1¼ yards plain linen, 45 inches wide

1¼ yards piping cord

18-inch square pillow form

8 Next take the inner flap. To make a neat hem, turn in ¼ inch along one of the long edges and press. Turn in another ¼ inch and press again. Machine stitch the hem in place.

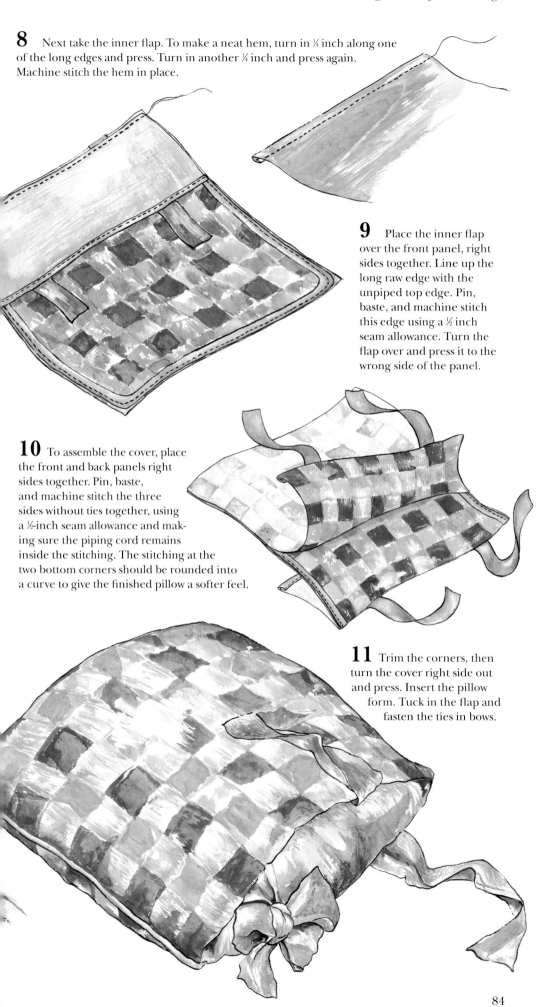

9 Place the inner flap over the front panel, right sides together. Line up the long raw edge with the unpiped top edge. Pin, baste, and machine stitch this edge using a ½ inch seam allowance. Turn the flap over and press it to the wrong side of the panel.

10 To assemble the cover, place the front and back panels right sides together. Pin, baste, and machine stitch the three sides without ties together, using a ½-inch seam allowance and making sure the piping cord remains inside the stitching. The stitching at the two bottom corners should be rounded into a curve to give the finished pillow a softer feel.

11 Trim the corners, then turn the cover right side out and press. Insert the pillow form. Tuck in the flap and fasten the ties in bows.

1 For the front and back cover, cut out two pieces of checked fabric measuring 19 x 19 inches. To make the inner flap, cut out one piece of plain linen measuring 8 x 19 inches and for the inner facing cut out one piece of plain linen measuring 2 x 19 inches. For the ties, cut out four strips of plain linen each 5½ x 13½ inches. Cut out enough plain linen to make 1¾ yards of piping (see Techniques, page 103).

2 To make the ties, fold each strip in half along the length with right sides together, and machine stitch along the raw edges of the long side and one of the short ends, using a seam allowance of ½ inch. Turn the ties right side out through the open end and press.

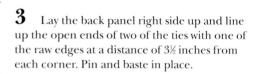

3 Lay the back panel right side up and line up the open ends of two of the ties with one of the raw edges at a distance of 3½ inches from each corner. Pin and baste in place.

4 Lay the narrow strip of inner facing over the ties, right sides facing, matching the raw edges. Pin, baste, and machine stitch along this edge through all layers, using a ½-inch seam allowance. Turn the facing over to the wrong side of the checked fabric and press.

5 Turn under a ¾-inch hem on the facing and machine stitch it down through all layers, making sure the stitching lines follow the line of the checks on the right side.

6 Place the front panel right side up. Place the remaining two ties along one of its raw edges, 3½ inches from each corner. Pin and then baste in place.

7 Lay the made-up piping along the other three sides of the right side of the front panel, lining up the raw edges. Pin, baste, and machine stitch close to the piping cord.

loose
linen cover

Two squares of cool striped beige linen with pairs of ties on each
side cover an inner pillow of contrasting striped fabric. A
simple-to-make pillow which will make a big impact, this idea is
excellent for giving a quick facelift to older pillows that
are looking a little "tired".

materials & equipment

⅔ yard beige striped linen fabric, 45 inches wide

⅝ yard red striped cotton fabric, 45 inches wide

5⅜ yards webbing or cotton tape in brown, 1 inch wide

5⅜ yards webbing or cotton tape in cream, ½ inch wide

18-inch square pillow form

5 To secure the ties to the cover, machine stitch as close as possible to the inner edge of the turned-in seam, sewing across each of the ties. Make sure that the ties are straight.

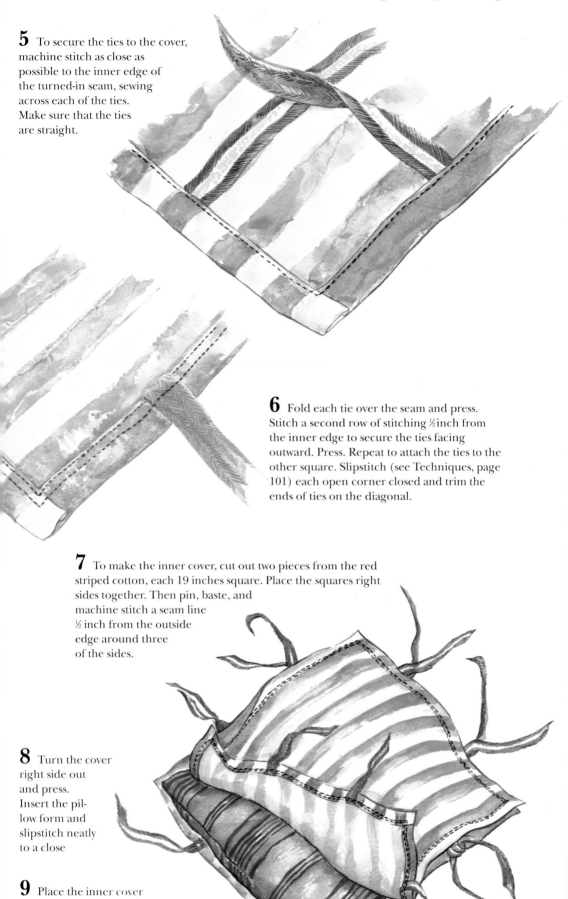

6 Fold each tie over the seam and press. Stitch a second row of stitching ½ inch from the inner edge to secure the ties facing outward. Press. Repeat to attach the ties to the other square. Slipstitch (see Techniques, page 101) each open corner closed and trim the ends of ties on the diagonal.

7 To make the inner cover, cut out two pieces from the red striped cotton, each 19 inches square. Place the squares right sides together. Then pin, baste, and machine stitch a seam line ½ inch from the outside edge around three of the sides.

8 Turn the cover right side out and press. Insert the pillow form and slipstitch neatly to a close

9 Place the inner cover in the middle of one outer panel (wrong side up), then put the other panel over it (wrong side down) and tie to close.

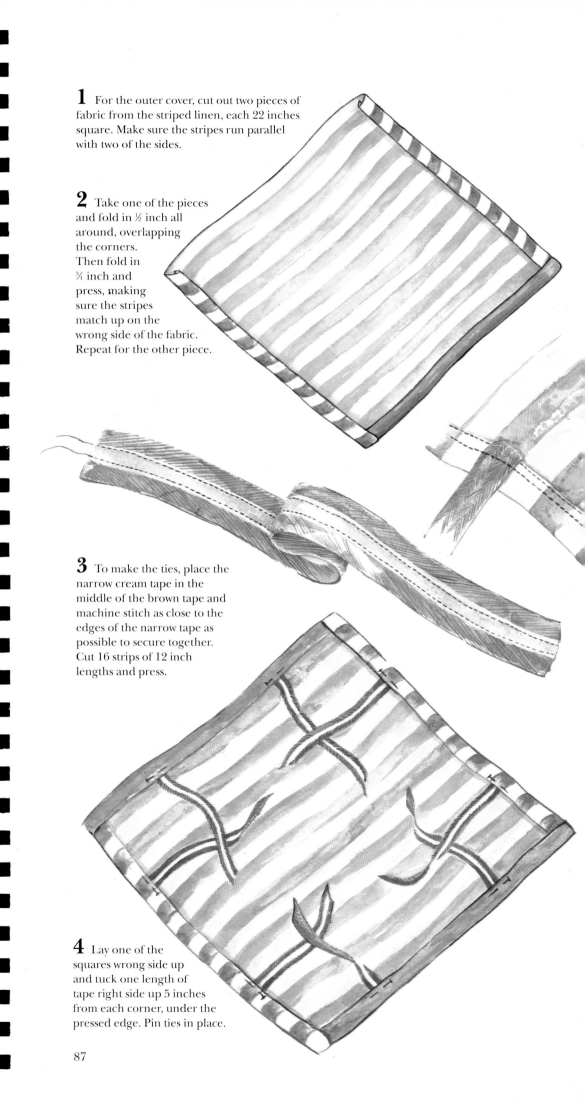

1 For the outer cover, cut out two pieces of fabric from the striped linen, each 22 inches square. Make sure the stripes run parallel with two of the sides.

2 Take one of the pieces and fold in ½ inch all around, overlapping the corners. Then fold in ¾ inch and press, making sure the stripes match up on the wrong side of the fabric. Repeat for the other piece.

3 To make the ties, place the narrow cream tape in the middle of the brown tape and machine stitch as close to the edges of the narrow tape as possible to secure together. Cut 16 strips of 12 inch lengths and press.

4 Lay one of the squares wrong side up and tuck one length of tape right side up 5 inches from each corner, under the pressed edge. Pin ties in place.

far left Hand-stitched parallel rows of white knitting yarn create a fine pattern on black wool.
left Black on white felt – painstakingly ordered circles have been cut out to provide the pattern on this white inner pillow.

surface decoration

For those who want to be challenged beyond running up pillows or covers on a sewing machine – or indeed for those who enjoy the slower pace of stitching by hand – there are numerous ways of applying surface decoration to your own or ready-made pillows. Cross stitch, embroidery, quilting pillows, and appliqué can all be used to add decorative and personal touches.

right A brown boiled wool cushion has been embroidered with charming naive multicolored flowers and finished with thick red rope piping.
below right Cream linen has been bordered in cross stitch in black embroidery thread; the back of the pillow is a contrasting checked gingham cotton.
below A corner detail of a wool and velvet ribbon patchwork pillow.

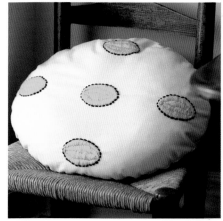

above A satin stitch embroidered heart in heavy yarn on fine cream flannel.
left from top Leftover fabrics and a carefully cut initial appliquéd together. Strong yellow ovals of yarn in satin stitch outlined in black. The most delicate flowers are intricately stiched onto cream linen. Hand-painted silk makes an elegant pillow. Embroidered leopard-skin needlepoint looks like the real thing!
below The brown knitted pillow has been tie-dyed and felted to give a unique finish, while the top pillow is a patchwork of velvet ribbon, knitted wool squares, and woven linen.

initials in cross stitch.

What could be more personal than working someone's initials into a cushion design? Cross stitch is extremely simple with lovely results. Here the cream edging on the scallops is echoed in the stitches. When you have decided on the initials you wish to stitch, make an accurate chart to refer to and count rigorously; the pattern is on page 104.

materials & equipment

⅝ yard brown evenweave linen, 45 inches wide

12 x 18-inch piece of cream felt

cream stranded embroidery floss

9 x 18-inch rectangular pillow form

graph paper, and patten paper

tapestry needle

compass

pinking shears

autumnal appliqué

Like many other forms of needlecraft, appliqué has survived for generations and lends itself particularly well to all manner of designs, pictorial or abstract. All you need to do is decide on a motif, or series of motifs, draw and cut them out from scraps of fabric, and apply them to a background. There is a template for the leaves on page 104.

materials & equipment

⅜ yard heavy cotton fabric, 45 inches wide

¼ yard contrasting fabric for the motif, 45 inches wide

¼ yard fusible bonding web, 45 inches wide

18-inch square pillow form

tracing paper

1 Cut two pieces of linen 10 x 19 inches and use one of these pieces as a base for the cross-stitch decoration. Trace the pattern onto graph paper and then transfer it to the center of the fabric (see Templates, page 104). Complete the design in cross stitch using cream floss.

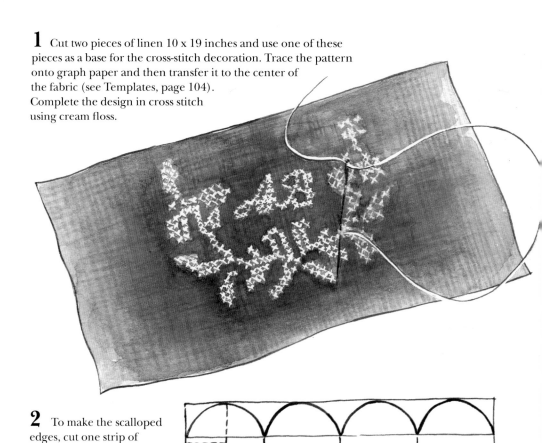

2 To make the scalloped edges, cut one strip of brown linen measuring 6 x 19 inches and two strips of felt measuring 6 x 18 inches. Make a template on a piece of pattern paper 3 x 19 inches. Draw four part-circles along the top of the paper with a 4⅜-inch diameter. Mark a point 1½ inches from the bottom edge between each circle; draw a straight line through the points. To make the scallops, cut out the outline of the top half of each circle.

3 Take the linen strip and fold it in half lengthwise, wrong sides together. Lay the template over it, lining up the long straight edge with the long raw edges of the fabric, and pin it down. Cut out the shapes, remove the paper, and clip between the scallops. Turn under ½ inch along the curves and the two short ends of the strips and press.

4 Fold the felt strips in half lengthwise and place a linen piece on top of each one. Pin, baste, and zigzag stitch the pieces together along the edge of the linen around the scallops and the short ends, (see Techniques, page 102).

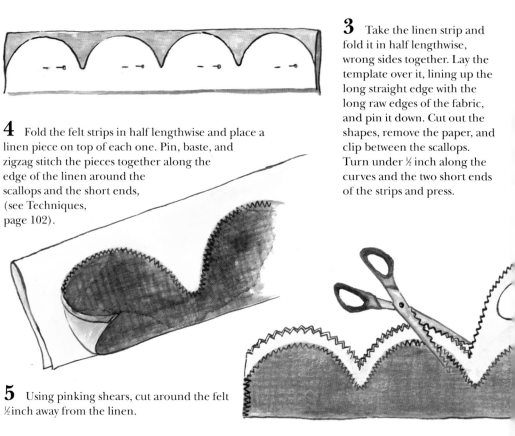

5 Using pinking shears, cut around the felt ½ inch away from the linen.

93

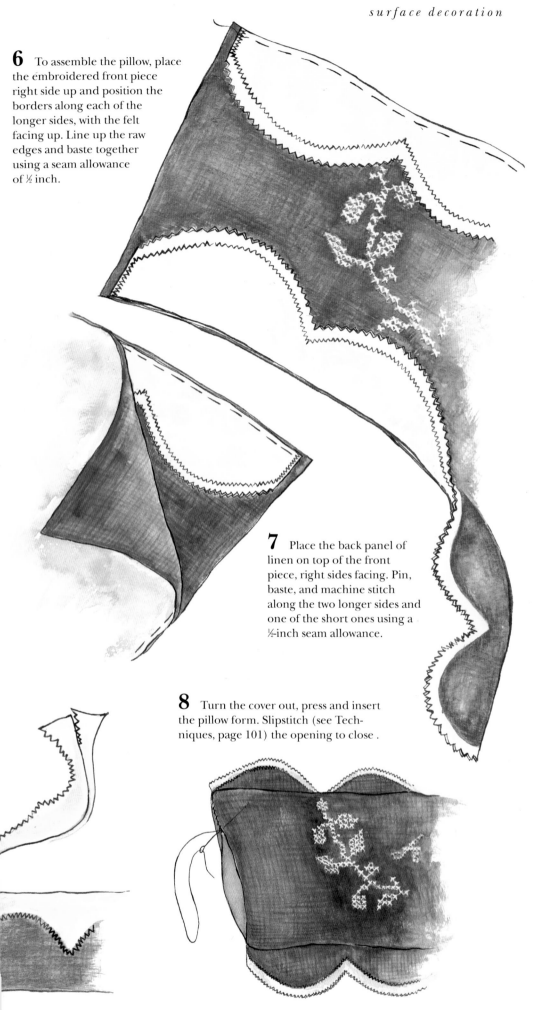

6 To assemble the pillow, place the embroidered front piece right side up and position the borders along each of the longer sides, with the felt facing up. Line up the raw edges and baste together using a seam allowance of ½ inch.

7 Place the back panel of linen on top of the front piece, right sides facing. Pin, baste, and machine stitch along the two longer sides and one of the short ones using a ½-inch seam allowance.

8 Turn the cover out, press and insert the pillow form. Slipstitch (see Techniques, page 101) the opening to close.

equipment and techniques

Sewing Kit

For the projects in this book you will need some basic tools. A few good scissors, including a pair of large, cutting-out shears, medium-size dressmaker's scissors, and small embroidery scissors for snipping threads. Pinking shears are useful for finishing raw edges and making decorative edgings. Use good-quality steel dressmaking pins which will not rust or go blunt: keep them in a box so they stay sharp. Choose your needle according to the weight of the fabric and the thickness of the thread and use a special needle for embroidery. An iron is invaluable during the making-up process but should be used with a damp cloth to protect delicate fabrics. Other useful items to have to hand are a seam ripper to unpick seams, a blunt knitting needle or pair of tweezers for pushing out corners, and a thimble.

Measuring and Marking Tools

Use a long, straight ruler together with a tape measure and double check all measurements. When it comes to drawing up circular or star shapes and smooth curves use a compass and protractor or a length of string attached to a pencil at one end with a pin at the other to act as a pivot. For specific designs that need to be scaled up and down, use graph paper, and you can purchase special paper for cutting out templates. When marking up a fabric, dressmaker's chalk is easy to apply and remove and comes in a variety of colors to suit your fabric; alternatively use contrasting basting cotton to make several small, loose loops which can be snipped away without trace. If you use a removable marker pen test it first to ensure it leaves absolutely no mark on the right side of the fabric.

Fabrics

In each project the fabrics are specified, as the weight, texture and pattern is suited to the particular design. Stick to a similar weight of fabric if you choose an alternative. Choose the type of fabric according to the function of the pillow. Use general furnishing fabrics for most pillows, tougher cloth for floor, outdoor or cushions and delicate fabrics for more decorative pillows. Check how much a fabric is likely to shrink as you may need to buy up to a third more material to compensate for this; if possible pick a colorfast cloth. Machine wash the fabric to pre-shrink it before starting the project, in case different sections shrink at different rates. For borders and back panels of pillows you can join sections of fabric that are not quite large enough by carefully matching up the pattern.

Pads and Fillings

Ready-made pillow forms come in a variety of shapes and sizes and with different fillings. The most luxurious filling is feather and down, which should be used sparingly in a puffy scatter pillow or more densely to stuff a firm seat cover. If you make your own pillow form with a feather filling use a downproof fabric such as a thick, close-weave cotton or sharp feather ends will protrude. Plain cotton or calico fabric is suitable for use with polyester fiber filling. Do not allow feather or synthetic pillows to get wet as they are very absorbent. Plastic or latex foam chips are lumpy and uncomfortable but non-absorbent and so useful for outdoor furnishings. Foam blocks can be cut to size and are used to form cushions for seating; cover the blocks with batting first to smooth out the corners.

1 Cut out two pieces of the heavy cotton fabric, each measuring 19 x 19 inches, for the front and back panels. Make sure the grain of the fabric is straight, not diagonal.

2 Place the piece of contrasting fabric over the fusible web and bond with an iron, following package instructions. Cut out four squares to fit the leaf motifs (see Templates, page 104).

3 Draw the shapes of the appliqué leaf motifs on the tracing paper, increasing the proportions to the desired size. Cut them out, and lay them over the contrasting fabric squares. Secure them in place with pins and carefully cut out each leaf.

4 Remove the backing and adhere the leaves to the right side of one of the cotton pieces. Topstitch them in place, close to the edges.

5 To decorate the leaves, machine stitch the outline of the veins and the stalks in a different colored thread using a tight zigzag stitch.

6 To assemble the cover, lay the remaining piece of cotton over the appliquéd piece, with right sides together. Pin, baste, and machine stitch along three sides, using a seam allowance of ½ inch.

7 Turn right side out, insert the pillow form and slipstitch (see Techniques, page 101) the ~n end closed .

98

SEWING TECHNIQUES

The sewing techniques in the projects featured involve both hand and machine stitches; the more complicated ones are outlined below. All the pillows can be completed however by using a back stitch. When marking and measuring fabric make sure you work in either imperial or metric.

Running or Gathering Stitch

A series of small, neat stitches, equal in length on both sides of the fabric. Running stitch is used to gather cloth by hand. Knot the thread at one end and sew two parallel rows of running stitches close together along the length to be gathered. Wind the loose threads at the other end around a pin and pull gently to form even gathers.

Slip Stitch

A simple way to join two folded edges. Knot the endof the thread and working from right to left insert the needle and slip it through the fold for about ¼ inch. On the other piece of fabric pick up a couple of threads to join the two edges. The stitches should be almost invisible, so keep them small. Slip stitch is easy to unpick if, say, you want to remove a pillow cover for washing.

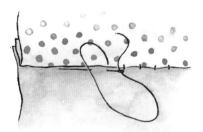

Hem Stitch

Use this stitch to hold a folded edge to flat fabric. Sewing a hem by hand produces a much neater result than machine hemming. On the wrong side catch a couple of threads from the flat fabric; with the needle pointing diagonally from right to left slide it under the folded edge and bring it up through both layers of the fold. Most hems are turned under twice, but for heavy fabrics make a single turn, after finishing the exposed raw edge (see page 102).

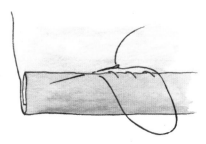

Back stitch

This creates a sturdy seam that can be used as an alternative to machine stitching, or for finishing thread ends securely by sewing a few stitches on top of one another, as an alternative to making a knot. After completing a stitch insert the needle at the end of the previous stitch, bring it out a stitch length in front of the thread to create a solid line of stitching on the right side and an overlapping effect on the underside.

Cross Stitch

Where possible, work decorative cross stitches in a line, first stitching half the cross before returning back along the line to complete the stitch. Make sure that the top stitches of the crosses all slant in the same direction.

Feather Stitch

Work this decorative stitch on the right side of the fabric. Bring the needle through at A, insert at B, bring through again at C, looping the thread under the needle before pulling it through. Mirror the process by inserting the needle at D, coming out at E and looping the thread under the needle once again. Repeat this pattern, alternating the looped stitches on either side off the central line.

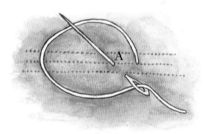

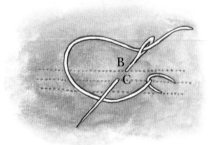

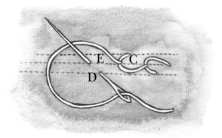

Blanket Stitch

A decorative stitch for neatening edges. Secure the thread at one end of the fabric and working from right to left insert the needle about ½inch from the edge; keep the thread under the point of the needle and complete the stitch to create a loop. Continue to work the stitches every ½inch or so, making sure the height is even.

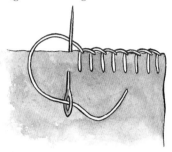

Buttonhole Stitch

This stitch is both decorative and strengthening as it prevents fraying of the cut to accommodate the button. Some machines have a buttonhole stitch attachment. Work on the right side using a short needle and a strong thread with a knotted end. Hide the knot on the wrong side of the fabric and work with the cut edge on the right (on the left if you are left-handed). Insert the needle at right angles to the cut edge, taking a stitch through the fabric, loop the thread behind the needle before pulling through to form a knot on the cut edge with each stitch. Keep the stitches evenly spaced, maintain an even tension on each knot and aim for the knots to touch each other. Fan the stitches close together around both ends of the hole, to prevent tearing. The more the fabric frays the deeper your stitches should be.

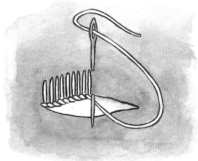

Seams

Stitch seams from top to bottom, making sure that patterned fabrics run the same way on either side of the join. The most commonly used seam is the flat seam; place the fabric right sides together with raw edges matching and pin, baste, and machine stitch to join, making a few backstitches to secure the threads at the end. For heavy fabrics trim the seam allowance close to the stitching to reduce bulk. If the seam is to be pressed to one side use a grading technique by cutting only one seam allowance back to create a smoother surface on the right side of the material. If the cloth is likely to fray finish the raw edges (see below).

Finishing Seams

There are three ways to finish seams to neaten and strengthen them. On fabric which is not liable to fray, you can either leave the seam allowance untrimmed, although you should neaten the corners (see below), or else pink the raw edges with pinking shears. To finish a seam by hand use oversewing or overcasting. To finish a raw edge by machine you can use a small and narrow zigzag, working the zigzag part over the raw edge or overlock with a serger.

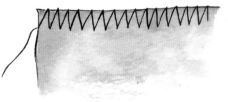

Neatening Corners and Curves

Although it is not strictly necessary to finish seams as the allowances lie inside the pillow cover and are not visible, for good results you should pay some attention to corners and curves. To create a neat pointed corner, stitch right up to the corner, leave the needle in the fabric, raise the machine foot and pivot the fabric through 90°, then lower the foot and continue stitching. Trim the seam allowance across the corner so you can push the finished corner out to a neat point. For sharp angles (such as the star project on page 12) machine one or two stitches across the point to strengthen it.

When sewing a curved seam keep a uniform seam allowance. For concave (inward-facing) curves snip little notches to achieve a flat finish. For convex (outward-facing) curves cut small slits into the seam allowance.

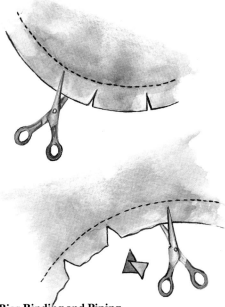

Bias Binding and Piping

Bias binding is the term given to strips of fabric cut on the diagonal grain that is used to cover piping cord. Both bias binding and piping cord are available ready-made but you can create much more versatile matching or contrasting trimmings yourself by making up your own. Choose a fabric of the same type and weight as the body of the pillow to avoid problems of shrinking and bunching after washing. Flat piping refers to a bias strip used folded in half without the cord inserted. Piping cord is available in different thickness, so choose an appropriate width. For safety, wash cotton cord before you begin sewing to pre-shrink it, or the piping may pucker later. Likewise, make sure that purchased piping and bias binding are shrinkproof and color-fast before sewing. To make bias strips, take a square of fabric and fold a straight raw edge parallel to the selvedge (the non-fray woven edge) to form a triangle. The bottom of the triangle is the bias line. Use a long ruler and dressmaker's chalk to mark out a series of lines parallel to the bias line, according to the width you require. Calculate the length of piping required and join enough strips to cover the cord. The bias must be wide enough to cover the cord comfortably with an additional ½ inch seam allowance.

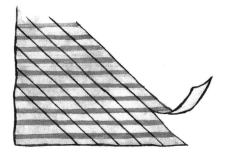

Cut out and join bias strips right sides together along the short ends with a flat seam. Press the seam and trim the corners to lie flat with the bias strip.

Place the bias strip wrong side up and fold evenly in half around the piping cord. Pin and baste to close, then machine or use back stitch (see page 101) to secure.

Apply the piping along the seam line between two pieces of fabric. Snip the seam allowance on the bias strip up to the stitching to help turn corners. Where the piped edges meet trim down the cord so the ends butt together and trim the fabric strip so there is an overlap of ½ inch; turn under one end for ½ inch and tuck the opposite raw edge inside; stitch across the join.

Transferring a Design

If your pattern is actual size it can be traced directly onto the tracing and transfer paper. If it has to be enlarged transfer the pattern onto graph paper and increase the proportion to the desired size; alternatively use a photocopier to enlarge. After you have done this rule horizontal and vertical lines through the center of the design. To transfer a design onto the front of a pillow cover, iron the piece of cloth you are going to embroider on and fold it in half vertically. Open out the fold and sew a straight line of basting stitches down the middle. Repeat to divide and mark the cloth in half along the horizontal to give you a guide for plotting the pattern. Use transfer paper or special dressmaker's carbon which is a non-smudge carbon paper that comes in several colors and is available from most haberdashers. Choose a paper that contrasts well with the fabric you are going to embroider on so that the design shows up clearly. Place the fabric right side up on a hard surface and place the transfer paper shiny side down over it. Place the tracing paper over the transfer paper and line up the horizontal and vertical lines already marked before pinning all three

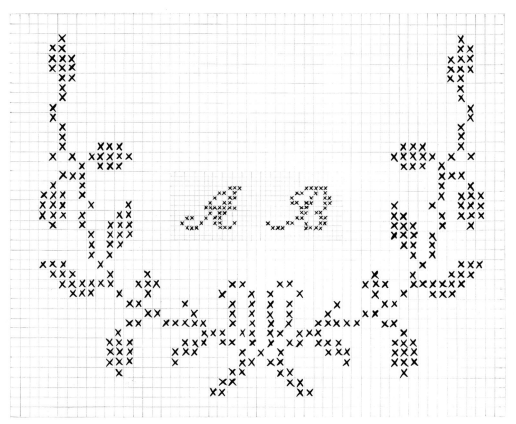

layers together. Trace over the design with a ballpoint pen or a pencil. Carefully remove the tracing and transfer papers and begin to cross stitch (see page 101) following the imprint of the design left on the fabric. Always work from the center outwards, as marked previously. The cross stitches should extend slightly beyond the carbon paper lines so they are not visible on the finished fabric. Remove the basting stitches once the embroidery is complete.

For the design above, (featured in the initials in cross stitch project, page 92) it is necessary to double the size of the pattern before transferring it to the fabric; use one of the methods explained earlier in Transferring a Design. To add a personal touch to your embroidered pillow insert the initials of your choice instead of using the ones given. To do this, leave a gap where the A and the B are and replace them with small crosses marking your new letters .

Use these two templates for the autumnal appliqué project featured on page 96; they must be doubled in size (see Transferring a Design, page 103) before being used to cut out the fabric.

suppliers

fabrics and trimmings

Laura Ashley
414 Madison Avenue,
New York, NY 10021

Beacon Hill
979 Third Avenue,
New York, NY 10022

Bennison Fabrics
76 Greene Street,
New York, NY 10012

*Boussac of France
979 Third Avenue,
New York, NY 10022

*Alan Campbell
979 Third Avenue,
New York, NY 10022

*Manuel Canovas
979 Third Avenue,
New York, NY 10022

Clarence House
211 East 58th Street,
New York, NY 10022

*Jane Churchill
Fabrics & Wallpapers
distributed by
Cowtan & Tout,
979 Third Avenue,
New York, NY 10022

*Colefax & Fowler
distributed by

Cowtan & Tout,
979 Third Avenue,
New York, NY 10022

*Coraggio Textiles
979 Third Avenue,
New York, NY 10022

*Cowtan & Tout
979 Third Avenue,
New York, NY 10022

Pierre Deux
870 Madison Avenue,
New York, NY 10003

*Designers Guild
distributed by Osborne &
Little, 979 Third Avenue,
New York, NY 10022

*Donghia
979 Third Avenue,
New York, NY 10022

*Decorator's Walk
979 Third Avenue,
New York, NY 10022

*Fortuny
979 Third Avenue,
New York, NY 10022

*Pierre Frey
distributed by Fonthill,
979 Third Avenue,
New York, NY 10022

Giant Textiles

P.O. Box 84228,
Seattle, WA 98124

***S.Harris & Co.
/Fabricut**
979 Third Avenue,
New York, NY 10022

*Hinson & Co.
979 Third Avenue,
New York, NY 10022

*Christopher Hyland
979 Third Avenue,
New York, NY 10022

*Lee Jofa
979 Third Avenue,
New York, NY 10022

***Kirk-Brummel
Associates**
979 Third Avenue,
New York, NY 10022

*Kravet Fabrics Inc.
979 Third Avenue,
New York, NY 10022

*Calvin Klein Home
654 Madison Avenue,
New York, NY 10022

Ralph Lauren Home
*979 Third Avenue,
New York, NY 10022
980 Madison Avenue,
New York, NY 10021
867 Madison Avenue,

New York, NY 10021

Jack Lenor Larsen
41 East 11th Street,
New York, NY 1003-4685

*Osborne & Little
979 Third Avenue,
New York, NY 10022

*Payne Fabrics, Inc.
979 Third Avenue,
New York, NY 10022

Ian Mankin at
Coconut Co.
129-31 Greene Street,
New York NY 10012-8080

*Quadrille Wallpapers
& Fabrics
979 Third Avenue,
New York, NY 10022

Randolph & Hein
1 Arkansas Street,
San Francisco, CA 94107

*Sanderson
979 Third Avenue,
New York, NY 10022

Scalamandre
942 Third Avenue,

New York, NY 10022

Schumacher Intl. Ltd.
939 Third Avenue,
New York, 10022

J.Robert Scott
& Associates
979 Third Avenue,
New York, NY 10022

Sonia's Place
979 Third Avenue,
New York, NY 10022

Stroheim & Romann
31 Thomson Avenue,
Long Island City, NY
11101

Jim Thompson/Zimmer
Rohde
979 Third Avenue,
New York, NY 10022

Westgate Fabrics
979 Third Avenue,
New York, NY 10022

pillows

A.B.C. Carpet & Home
888 Broadway,
New York, NY 10011

Bloomingdales
1000 Third Avenue,
New York, NY 10022

Gracious Homes
1220 Third Avenue.
New York, NY 10021

Charlotte Moss
1027 Lexington Avenue
New York, NY 10011

*Nicolas
979 Third Avenue
New York, NY 10012

The Pillowry
1132 East 61st Street,
New York, NY 10021

*Pillow Finery
979 Third Avenue
New York, NY 10022

*John Rosselli
523 East 73rd Street
New York, NY 10021

*indicates trade only:
contact the address
givento find out your
nearest supplier

credits

Front cover picture: from top to bottom: fabric by Schumacher from Turnell & Gigon; inner fabric from Liberty, outer fabric from John Lewis; fabric from Nobilis Fontan, trimming from V. V. Rouleaux; fabric from Designers Guild, trimming from V. V. Rouleaux; fabric from Nobilis Fontan

page 1 from left to right: pillow from Liberty; fabric from Colefax & Fowler; pillow made by Hikaru Noguchi

page 2 from top to bottom: pillow from Liberty; pillow made by Hikaru Noguchi; fabric from Manuel Canovas; silk fron JAB; tweed from Liberty

page 4 from left to right: pillow made by Celia Dewes; fabric from Turnell & Gigon; fabric by Schumacher from Turnell & Gigon, tassel from Wendy Cushing

page 5 from left to right: fabric from Chelsea Textiles; fabric from Chelsea Textiles, trimmings by V. V. Rouleaux; fabric from Colefax & Fowler, trimmings by V. V. Rouleaux

page 6 fabric from John Lewis, trimmings by V. V. Rouleaux

page 7 all pillows from Cath Kidston

page 8 from top to bottom: fabric from Parkertex, trimming from Osborne & Little; fabric from Colefax & Fowler; fabric from Chelsea Textiles Churchill; fabric from Sanderson, edging fabric from Osborne & Little

page 9 from top to bottom: fabric from Colefax & Fowler; fabric from Parkertex, piping from Firifiss; fabric from Sanderson, trimming from Jane Churchill

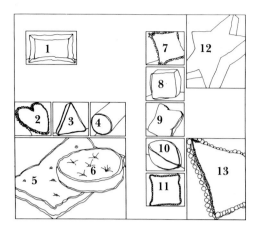

shapes pages 10-11

1 striped fabric from Sanderson, outer fabric from Osborne & Little

2 fabric from Parkertex, trimming from Osborne & Little

3 fabric from Parkertex, piping from Firifiss

4, 5, 9, 11 fabric from Colefax & Fowler

6, 8, 10 fabric from Osborne & Little

7 fabric from Parkertex, trimming from Jane Churchill

12 fabric from Chelsea Textiles

13 fabric from Sanderson, trimming from Jane Churchill

projects: *the star:* fabric from Chelsea Textiles • *bee bolster:* fabric from Chelsea Textiles • *striped tufted mattress:* fabric by Schumacher from Turnell & Gigon • *ball fringe in the round:* fabric from The Conran Shop, ball fringe from Jane Churchill

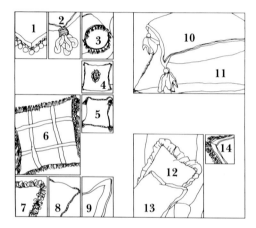

use of fabrics pages 28-29

1 fabric from Colefax & Fowler, trimming by Nina Campbell from Osborne & Little

2 pillow made by Hikaru Noguchi

3 pillow from Mulberry

4 pillow from William Yeoward

5, 6, 8, 10, 11 pillows from Harrods

7 fabric from Zoffany, trimming from Osborne & Little

9 fabric from Liberty

12, 13 fabrics from B. Brown

14 pillow from Linda Gumb

projects: *stripes into squares:* fabric by Schumacher from Turnell & Gigon, tassel from Wendy Cushing • *basket weave of ribbons:* made by Hikaru Noguchi • *patchwork puzzle:* antique • *floppy stone-washed silk:* fabric from Alton-Brooke

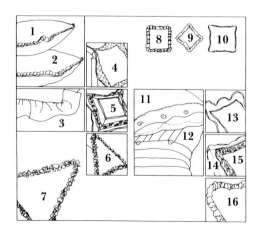

borders and edgings pages 46-47

1, 2 fleece and thread from John Lewis

3 both fabrics from Sanderson

4 printed fabric from Colefax & Fowler, red fabric from Parkertex, embroidery linen from John Lewis

5 pillow from The Blue Door

6, 7 fabric from John Lewis, trimming from V. V. Rouleaux

8 fabrics from John Lewis

9 fabric and bias binding from John Lewis

10 pillow from John Lewis

11, 12, 15 pillows from The Blue Door

13 fabric from The Blue Door

14 pillow from Tobias & the Angel

16 fabric from Monkwell

projects: *scallops and zigzags:* fabrics from John Lewis • *box-pleated border:* fabric from Sahco Hesslein • *double-ruffle taffeta:* fabric from Pierre Frey • *double-flanged border:* fabrics from G.P. & J. Baker

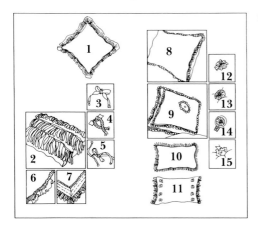

trimmings and fastenings pages 64-65

1 fabric and trimmings from John Lewis
2 trimming from V. V. Rouleaux
3 fabric from Monkwell
4 fabric by Schumacher from Turnell & Gigon
5 fabric from The Blue Door
6 fabric from JAB, trimming from V. V. Rouleaux
7 fabric from The Conran Shop, trimming from Wendy Cushing
8 pillow from Chelsea Textiles
9 fabric from Osborne & Little, trimming from V. V. Rouleaux
10 fabric from Sahco Hesslein, trimming from Sanderson
11 fabric from John Lewis, trimmings from Sanderson
12, 13 tufts from Colefax & Fowler
14 antique button
15 fabric from Colefax & Fowler

projects: *rope-edged knotted pillow:* inspired by Wendy Harrop, fabric from Ian Mankin, rope border from John Lewis • *fastened with tassels:* inner fabric from Manuel Canovas, outer fabric from John Lewis, tassels from Wendy Cushing • *the envolope pillow:* fabric from Sanderson, trimmings from John Lewis • *all trimmed:* fabric from Colefax & Fowler, trimmings from V.V. Rouleaux • *checked linen with contrast ties:* check fabric by Schumacher from Turnell & Gigon, plain from John Lewis • *linen slipcover:* fabrics from Sanderson, ties from John Lewis

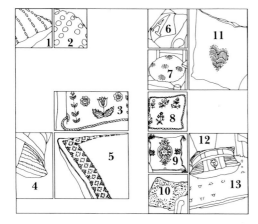

surface decoration pages 90-91

1, 7 fabric and trimmings from John Lewis
2 pillow from Margret Adolfsdottir
3, 10 pillow from Cath Kidston
4, 12 pillow by Hikaru Noguchi from Timney & Fowler
5 pillow embroidered by Gillian Bowden
6 spotted fabric from Designers Guild, striped fabric from Hodsoll McKenzie
8 pillow from Chelsea Textiles
9 pillows from Harrods
11 pillow made by Celia Dewes
13 pillow by Jo Sheffield

projects: *initials in cross stitch:* fabric from Manuel Canovas, felt from B. Brown • *autumnal appliqué:* fabrics from John Lewis

page 100 pillow from The Blue Door
page 105 from top to bottom: fabric from The Conran Shop; silk from JAB; pillow from Liberty; fabric from Zoffany, trimming by Nina Campbell at Osborne & Little; fabric from Osborne & Little, trimming from V. V. Rouleaux
page 106 from left to right: fabric by Schumacher from Turnell & Gigon, tassels from Henry Newbery; fabric from Zoffany, tassels from Wendy Cushing
page 110 fabric from John Lewis; fringe and tufted buttons from Sanderson
page 111 antique pillow from Antiques & Things
page 112 pillow by Hikaru Noguchi from Timney Fowler
endpapers: all fabrics from John Lewis; top trimming V. V. Rouleaux, all others from John Lewis

glossary

Basting
Large straight stitches used to fasten fabric temporarily.

Batting
Soft, pliable cotton or synthetic lining or filling material.

Bonding web
Paper-backed sticky material attached to fabric for added strength.

Braid
A woven ribbon used to trim or edge pillows and cushions.

Carpet webbing
Strong closely woven tape used to support upholstery or cut into lengths to form ties.

Chenille
Tufty and soft velvety yarn; wool, cotton, or synthetic.

Cotton
A natural fiber made from the boll of the cotton plant, producing strong and durable yarn.

Crewel work
Large-scale embroidery

Damask
A reversible figured woven fabric, usually silk, satin, or linen.

Drawn thread work
Ornamental work done by removing threads in one direction and grouping the rest with a thicker thread.

Facing
A section of material added for strength or contrast.

Felt
Unwoven cloth made from pounded wool; the edges do not fray when they are cutg.

Figured material
Fabric with a pattern, formed by the weave structure.

Filo floss
A six-stranded plied silk thread.

Flange
A projecting flat rim or border.

Gathers
Puckers or folds made in cloth by drawing on a loosely stitched thread.

Gaufrage
A pattern branded onto the surface of velvet.

Gauze
A sheer, strong but delicately woven fabric.

Interlining
Soft material, used as backing or inner lining.

Kapok
Fluffy, fine stuffing material

Knife pleat
A narrow flat pleat.

Linen
Fiber spun from flax to produce a thick and flexible fabric.

Madras cotton
Striped and checked fine Indian cotton, usually in bright colors.

Miter
The diagonal joining of two pieces of fabric at a corner.

Organdy
A fine, sheer and crisp fabric made with cotton yarns.

Organza
A thin, plain-woven silk or synthetic fabric with a stiff finish.

Provençal print
French country prints on cotton, characterized by small brightly colored motifs.

Raw edge
The cut edge of fabric, without selvage or hem, which often needs finishing to prevent them from fraying.

Satin
Silk, cotton, or synthetic fabric with a smooth, glossy surface and a dull back.

Satin Stitch
An embroidery stitch used to fill a design.

Seam allowance
The narrow strip of raw-edged fabric left when making a seam, to allow for fraying.

Seam line
The line formed when two pieces of material are stitched together.

Selvage
The defined warp edge of the fabric, specially woven to prevent unraveling.

Silk
Luxurious, strong fabric produced by silkworms.

Squab
A thick box-shaped pillow form.

Stone-washed silk
Faded silk produced by washing with abrasives.

Stranded floss
A six-stranded thread with a sheen; used for embroidery.

Template
A cardboard or paper shape, used to mark outlines on fabric.

Tie-dyed cloth
A texture and pattern produced after resist printing.

Toile
Plain cloth on its own or in *Toile de Jouy* to mean fabric embellished with pictorial scenes.

Topstitch
A straight seam that shows on the right side of the fabric.

Velvet
A rich fabric, usually made of cotton or synthetic fiber, with a thick and soft warp-pile.

Weave
An interlacing action used to form something such as a fabric.

Width
The distance from selvage to selvage on any fabric. The usual widths are 36 inches, 45 inches and 60 inches.

index

acknowledgements

Without the goodwill, trust, and kindness of the press offices of all the fabric suppliers mentioned in the credits we would not have had very much to photograph for this book; to you all, many thanks. All at Ryland Peters & Small who have worked hard on this project, especially Jacqui, Anne, David, Ingunn, Sophie and Sian – what a team! James Merrell's unflagging enthusiasm and gorgeous pictures are always appreciated.

Heartfelt thanks go to Catherine Coombes, who has not only been an invaluable assistant, but has also held together the homefront during shoots; always with a positive, sweet, and cheery disposition. Thanks go also to the kind people who let us use their homes to photograph in, and to all the people who helped by lending goods or being otherwise helpful during this project: Isobel Bird, Trudi Ballard, Gillian Bowden, Celia Dewes, Cath Kidston, Angel Hughes, Catharina Mannerfelt, Hikaru Noguchi, Annie Stevens, and Susie Tinsley.

And finally thanks to my boys; David, my husband, Harry, our son, and Rufus the family mutt.

dedication

For Hänsi Schneider, with love and gratitude